CHRIST AND
THE HUMAN PROSPECT

By the same author

Letters to an Ordinand
Mary and the Christian Gospel

John de Satgé

CHRIST AND THE HUMAN PROSPECT

The Unity of Existence Here and Hereafter

LONDON
SPCK

First published 1978
SPCK
Holy Trinity Church
Marylebone Road
London NW1 4DU

Filmset in Great Britain by
Northumberland Press Ltd, Gateshead Tyne and Wear
and printed by
Fletcher and Son Ltd, Norwich

ISBN 0 281 03631 4

In piam memoriam
JOHANNIS GEORGII STOBBART
presbyteri docti
soceri dilecti

Contents

Acknowledgements

Thanks are due to the following for permission to quote from copyright sources:

The Revd Walter M. Abbott, s.j., Geoffrey Chapman Publishers, and The America Press: *The Documents of Vatican II*, edited by Walter M. Abbott, s.j.

The Literary Executors of the late Gilbert Shaw: Essay by Gilbert Shaw in *Angels of Light and Powers of Darkness*, edited by E. L. Mascall.

The Book of Common Prayer of 1662 is Crown copyright and extracts used herein are with permission.

Quotations from the Revised Standard Version of the Bible, copyrighted 1946, 1952, © 1971, 1973 by the Division of Christian Education of the National Council of the Churches of Christ in the USA, are used by permission.

I

The Starting Point

Theology does not leave its students unchanged, as I found when I drew together a number of occasional writings and a great volume of notes on Mariology, an ecumenical interest of many years standing. To my surprise, I found that I had become personally involved. The Mariology which emerged from the Second Vatican Council was not only compatible with Evangelical Christianity, but brought it positive enrichment. No sooner had I finished the first draft of *Mary and the Christian Gospel*[1] than the Papal Exhortation *Marialis Cultus* appeared,[2] banishing any fears that the directions decided upon by such a narrow majority at the Council[3] might be reversed. I was obliged, therefore, to modify the version of Christianity by which I had lived for a quarter of a century, expanding it to include devotion to the Lord's mother.

A change of that magnitude does not happen in isolation. The emotional consequences are considerable, for deep-seated prejudices are affected. Theologically, a shift of perspective makes newly unfamiliar the settled differences of Christendom. Questions long since considered settled demanded to be heard again, prickly matters such as indulgences and the treasury of the Church.

When a man knows he is to be hanged in a fortnight, it concentrates his mind wonderfully, said Dr Johnson.[4] So does a major shift in personal convictions. Matters of Mariology, the communion of saints, and so on, all involved taking seriously the 'unseen world'. That was a matter to which I had never given much consideration; and in that, I suspect, I am not alone in my generation.

Today's religious teaching puts a heavy emphasis on this present world. Now is the day of salvation, now is the hour of judgement. Today we are to hear the Lord's voice, and it is in the here-and-now that the integrity of our profession stands or falls. The biblical theology which opposes the Hebraic doctrine of resurrection to Greek notions of immortality prefers to speak of a body ensouled than of body and soul. It has little to say about life beyond the present; and in its silence perhaps more than in its assertions it marches with the materialistic sides of science and technology.

And in so doing it has little to say to the ordinary needs of ordinary people; but more of that later.

Biblical theology slides easily into that theology of secularism which takes its Christianity religionless and on occasions celebrates the Death of God. But even those who express their belief in traditional forms share in the spirit of the age. It is easy to think of two spheres of existence: ours, which is set in time and space and the universe accessible to scientific inquiry; and God's, the divine realm of Father, Son, and Holy Spirit, the Ultimate Energy, the Beyond behind all that is created. So there is God and ourselves.

But other created beings outside our space and time? An almost Buddhist disposition of mind thinks of the faithful departed as assimilated to God (one does not say 'absorbed into God' since, as everyone knows, the universe is personal). Those who are finally unfaithful, if any, cease to be. The notion of a 'spiritual realm' is as unnecessary from the religious point of view as it is unacceptable philosophically.

But consider Mary not as a dead Jewess but as our Lady, as the human individual in whom the powers of her Son's redemption have worked to their full term of glory; consider her as someone who prays for her Son's people 'militant here in earth'; consider her in a peculiar but active sense as your mother; and all kinds of question immediately arise. Questions about the objective existence of a spiritual realm, about time and space, about history and the end, follow each other in relentless succession.

Extend the thought further. Open it to include 'a great multitude which no man could number, from every nation, from all tribes and peoples and tongues . . .'[5]

Consider also the angels.

This book attempts to co-ordinate some of these matters. It

explores certain areas of human experience here and hereafter as the Christian faith describes them; the areas of fellowship and communion, of 'common life in the Body of Christ'.[6]

It is an ecumenical exploration. Because the enterprise was provoked by a reassessment of teaching largely from the Roman Catholic Church, it looks to the teaching of that Church for possible light. But it starts from an Evangelical base and tries always to show the connection.

There are four principal chapters. 'The Edges of Mystery' maps out the territory, which is, of course, by no means all Christian. 'Adam from First to Last' sets the phenomenon of human existence in its environment. 'Jacob's Ladder' examines the ways in which the supernatural, divine and otherwise, impinges on the here-and-now.

The fourth chapter, 'Militant Here in Earth', is evidently set firmly in this present life. It suggests the ecumenical consequences of accepting the positions advanced in the previous chapters. It ought possibly to have been made into a book on its own, and indeed at one stage I had intended that. But in the end it seemed that the previous material would be less effective without strong roots in the present Christian scene.

2

The Edges of Mystery

I

'Christianity not mysterious', proclaimed John Toland, most flamboyant of Deists, in his title of 1696. Many theological works published in the 1960s and '70s might have envied that title.

But the differences are important. The Deists came at the end of the seventeenth century when all Europe was weary of religious strife. They came in the wake of that newly launched ship, the Royal Society. Science, with its modern principles of inference controlled by observation, had become respectable; no longer had the facts to fit into theories derived from religiously authenticated principles. Instead, the creation was found to exist in a marvellous unity, for religion in its essentials agreed with the facts of nature. The words of God in the Bible and his work in the earth and the sea and the stars were one.

> The spacious firmament on high
> With all the blue ethereal sky,
> And spangled heavens, a shining frame
> Their great Original proclaim.
> The unwearied sun from day to day
> Does his Creator's sun display,
> And publishes to every land
> The works of an almighty hand.[1]

Opinions were divided among English divines in the generation that followed the Glorious Revolution of 1688. Most of them drew deeply from the wells of Anglican tradition, the old Catholic religion strained through the Book of Common Prayer and the Thirty-nine Articles of Religion. The world of nature showed the handiwork of God, whose own nature was to be known through his Son Jesus Christ and so through the teaching of the Church which that Son had founded. But others, among whom Toland was a maverick and Matthew Tindal more representative, went further. Nature was all that mattered. The rest was intrusion: mystifying priestcraft, alien superstition, contributing nothing to the furtherance of virtue in human life, which was, of course, the true end of religion. Christianity was not mysterious.

Today's theologians are different. Coming after Marx and after Freud, they lack the innocence of the eighteenth century and are not so naive as to suppose that truth may be equated with common sense; human nature is not straightforward and simple. They (if it is possible thus to generalize; the theological avant-garde form even less of a coherent school than did the Deists) do not abandon mystery. They resite it. The mystery lies in human relationships, in the depths of a person and the interstices between person and person, in the reactions among groups. It is in the depths of human experience that we find the beyond of our midst. Mystery is no longer supernatural; the natural is surprisingly mysterious.

One consequence is widespread. The desire to locate deepest truth within the experiences of this present life often involves suspicion of any attempt to refer ultimate significance to a point beyond or outside the limits of empirically verifiable experience. It is here and now, or nowhere, that we meet God. Although there are some who style themselves 'Christian atheists', most of these theologians manage not only to find God exclusively in the depths of human experience, but also speak about him in ways which connect with many traditional Christian teachings.

Secular theologians (to use a convenient if loose term) are wise in relocating the mystery instead of abandoning it. But they are seriously misguided in their refusal to look also outside the circle of present experience.

2

In making that refusal, secular theologians are responding to one of the great pressures of contemporary opinion. They would no doubt agree with that judgement, insisting that such pressures themselves reflect God's will manifesting itself in the march of events. I do not share that confidence. But first we should stand back and view the matter in a long historical perspective.

Eighteenth-century theologians tried to teach a Christianity modified in accordance with a phase of scientific thought which placed great weight on the 'laws of nature'. Today's theologians work in a world which operates according to principles much further removed from any divine control. It is possible to retrace the course of a rearguard action fought by theologians intent upon finding a line beyond which scientific explanation gave place to religious. The nineteenth century saw hostility mounting between science and religion.

The extent of the hostility is not always realized. 'It is generally supposed that the Church flew into an unnecessary panic over the attempts of innocent and disinterested scientists to understand the secrets of the world', wrote an acute historian, Stephen Neill. Nothing, he insists, could be further from the truth.

In the closing decades of the nineteenth century the Christian faith was the object of unremitting, skilful, and malevolent attacks of enemies who wished for nothing more ardently than the total disappearance of that faith from the earth.[2]

Christian teachers tried, by finding points of contact, to combat the assumption that science had taken over. They endeavoured also to set limits to the autonomy of science: thus far and no further; beyond that, religion must explain. The latter enterprise resembled the legendary attempt of King Canute to turn back the waves, and secular theologians are right in not wishing to uphold some 'god of the gaps'. He is Lord of the whole or of nothing, and those who continue to believe in him must try to discern his face in the whole.

Secular theologians, then, are right to insist that whatever science can observe it must describe, and that theology can have no reserved areas. They are right also in adding a

6

theological description to the scientific; but they are wrong in supposing that there are no areas of existence other than those open now or in the future to scientific research. To assume so is to make an act of faith.

We may take the matter up from Disraeli's famous intervention in the Victorian war between religion and science. 'I am not prepared to say that the lecture-room is more scientific than the Church', he declared at Oxford on 25 November 1864.

> What is the question now placed before society with a glib assurance the most astounding? The question is this—Is man an ape or an angel? My Lord, I am on the side of the angels . . .[3]

Disraeli, Bishop Neill comments, had not merely coined a piquant and memorable phrase; 'he had summed up in a sentence what, in our own day, is still a major issue of faith or unbelief.'

Disraeli's choice of example has become even more apt in very recent years. A school of popular scientific writers have interpreted human behaviour by analogy with that of the higher apes; and while theologians have been notably coy on the subject of angels, more and more people outside church circles are trying to make contact with what they believe to be discarnate spirits.

3

The supernatural is often taken to be a form of scaffolding needed while the house of humanity is under construction; once the house is built, the scaffolding can only mark the design and must be taken down. Or it is a crutch to be thrown away when the leg is mended; or, most telling of all, the nightlight that burns to keep at bay the imaginary dangers of childhood.

Another line of contemporary thought about the supernatural connects it less with imperfection than with metaphor. Ranges of experience exist which can hardly be described. They may be spoken about in abstract terms; but all the world loves a story, and Jesus taught in parables. Supernatural talk is a signpost from outside pointing to an inner reality. It is absurd to value the signpost as if it were itself that to which it points.

There is of course some truth in both these views, and we do well to keep our life and discourse as far as possible within natural limits. One should interpret events by unusual explanations only when the usual ones have proved inadequate. Mankind has enormously increased his range of knowledge, and processes which not long ago would have seemed miraculous now lie within everyone's understanding.

We will consider later whether any areas remain which will never yield to explanation in terms of 'natural' life. But first let us examine a claim often made, that the dismissal of the supernatural is a means of liberating mankind and enriching human experience.

Up to a point, no doubt, it is. Who can look at a society where spirits at every turn demand propitiation and not believe that its people are the freer for the coming of education and science? Medicine, hygiene, dietary reform reduce the restrictive misery which the witchdoctor's craft engendered rather than cleared; even so the condition of such a society a few years later may remind one of the house that was left clean and empty, only to be occupied by squatters far more squalid than its previous occupants.

It is foolish to deny the advantages brought about by the application of science to human living. It is a false romanticism which looks back to the good old days and sees there a happier society. Criticism of the past is not confined to radicals or revolutionaries.

No portion of the European past has been subjected to more critical scrutiny than that which came to be known as the 'Age of Faith'. Historians, sociologists, psychologists even, have dissected the religious history of Europe, laying bare all its sordid details. Martin Luther has been interpreted in terms of constipation.[4] It is all part of a climate of opinion where religion is merely an aspect of human behaviour and a genuinely supernatural reference is not to be considered.

'Mankind has come of age.' Bonhoeffer's great phrase is used in senses which he might well not recognize. But is it true that mankind, having shaken off the childish things of religion, attained to maturity? Are we serene in our secularism, happy in our autonomy?

There is little in our high culture to suggest it. We have the theatre of the Absurd,[5] the politics of envy, the permissive morality. The message seems to be that the world is a bad job and we have to make the best of it. It is less a matter of living happily than of avoiding unhappiness. Forecasts are bleak though generally brave. The world is a paradox, claustrophobic with its threat of starvation or holocaust, yet limitless in its promise of space-travel. Perhaps never before have the moulders of opinion reflected so faithfully the hopeless vision of Thomas Hobbes:

> No arts; no letters; no society; and which is worst of all, continual fear and danger of violent death; and the life of man, solitary, poor, nasty, brutish, and short.[6]

Small wonder, then, that many attempts are made to escape from the closed world of boundless technological autonomy. Some people break into fields of altered perception, exploring inner space through meditation or drugs, despairing of the political activism which leads others to revolutionary endeavour. Others concern themselves with ancient arts, reviving the magic of the past, delving into the occult for some key with which to open doors into the unknown. Some people try to contact discarnate spirits in which they partly believe. Sages, prophets, *gurus* abound, the more exotic the better.

The religious situation in our culture today has curious parallels with that of the first Christian centuries, when the old Roman virtues had been shaken and confused by influences released among them by the success of the imperial venture. One might suppose therefore that the Christian gospel would have as ready a hearing now as it did then; for then too the human spirit was oppressed by alien forces, and its nerve was failing. In some parts of the world the gospel is indeed advancing with great speed, notably through the pentecostal movement.

But in general it is not so. Perhaps the chief difference between the first Christian century and our own is that then a

new and vigorous faith moved across a tired and dispirited
world. Now, in too many places, the faith is as tired and
dispirited as the world in which it is set. And so theologians
commit the treason of scaling down the faith they present to
the size which the world demands: a secular gospel for a secular
world. But, they ask, what else can they do? Are they not
moderns, as modern as those to whom they present the faith?
It is not they who calculate how much Jones can swallow; they
themselves are Jones, and their throats will not open wider.
Even the more robust Catholics and Evangelicals modify their
message in ways which their predecessors would have considered compromising, so assiduously do they strive to be
'relevant'.

Is there in fact something qualitatively different between this
generation and its predecessors? The authors of the Church of
England report *Christian Believing* (1976) appear to believe that
there is. They find a new element in the present situation.

> Our ancestors treated the [biblical and credal] texts in this
> way because they did believe that the similarities between
> the various ages of human history far outweighed any
> differences.... And this was plausible because until the
> sixteenth century the world-view of European man was
> indeed basically the same as that of the ancient cultures.
> The shattering changes in the understanding of reality that
> have marked the modern world have forced us to face the
> fact that man is an historical being, that he exists in a
> continuum of change, and that he cannot therefore take for
> granted that all ages and cultures shared his own principles
> and forms of thought.[7]

The Commission was evidently unable to decide how far the
'new element', 'the shattering changes in the understanding of
reality', affected the 'dialogue with' the past demanded by
responsible teaching today.

Ten years earlier Dr E. L. Mascall, an Anglican theologian
trained originally in mathematics and standing in the Thomist
tradition of orthodox Catholicism, had put it rather differently.

Human religions have indeed been of the most outstanding

variety, but, until the rise of modern secularism, it seems to have been natural to man to recognise that, behind and beyond the world that our senses perceive, there is another realm of being which, unlike the world of our senses, requires no explanation, and which, in some way or another, confers explanation upon the world of our senses and gives meaning to human life.[8]

The 'new element' perceived by the members of the Doctrine Commission seems to be the assumption held by so many theologians that this sense of 'another realm of being' has disappeared.

Marxists and 'the people who arrogate to themselves the title of scientific humanists' (Mascall's phrase) view the change as liberation, a breaking of the shackles of superstition. Dr Mascall, who is evidently sceptical (as I am) as to how far this change deeply affects people outside the circles of the theologically or atheistically articulate, finds a truer explanation of the phenomenon to be

> that our urbanized technocratic civilization has atrophied a faculty which is really natural to man, so that we have now become incapable, without a great deal of de-conditioning, of seeing something which is really under our noses and which was as plain as a pikestaff to our ancestors.[9]

He adds two pertinent observations. Belief in a world beyond that of our sense-experience is one of the things that distinguishes man from the animals; and where 'emancipation' from such belief has happened, the result has been not happiness and fulfilment but existentialist despair. G. K. Chesterton had made much the same point a generation earlier when he insisted that Catholicism was 'the only thing that frees a man from the degrading slavery of being a child of his age'.[10]

It is not necessary to share the Catholicism of Chesterton or even of Dr Mascall in order to applaud their refusal to be swept away by the tide of secular theology. Traditional Protestantism has held as firmly as traditional Catholicism to its belief in a supernatural world. There are fortunately many teachers and pastors who prefer the scorn of the sophisticated to the weakening of their own and their people's faith. J. B. Phillips, translator of the Bible, spoke for many when he wrote:

> I believe that by cutting out the whole realm of spiritual reality (of which this little life is a mere outcrop in time and space) we are robbing ourselves of more than we realise. Instead of being sons of God with unlimited potential when our present probation is over, we are merely decent humanists with a tinge of Christian piety.[11]

Assertions of this kind are neither a bigoted repetition of traditional beliefs which have no present-day validation, nor are they attempts to insulate believers from the cold winds of modern reality. Their appeal to an open-minded scholar who depends on no ecclesiastical commitment is shown strikingly in the American sociologist Peter Berger's book, *A Rumour of Angels*.[12] Berger complains that secular theology, like the neo-orthodoxy from which it sprang, has reacted too far against the theological liberalism that preceded it. Particularly unfortunate is the neglect of human experience as a principal, if not *the* principal, source for theological construction. Christianity fails to communicate with the modern world precisely because it does not emphasize those 'signals of transcendence' which are present for all to see in the most ordinary human behaviour. He describes those 'signals' as they are found in the belief in orderliness, in play, in hope (and in its opposite, the belief that damnation is possible), and in humour.

Professor Berger is no advocate of a return to theological conservatism, Protestant or Catholic. He wishes rather to find in the humanistic disciplines a series of pointers leading beyond everyday experience to something which could be called a natural theology; only after 'discovery' will he allow 'revelation.' He wishes then to 'confront' the established religious traditions with that natural theology or inductive faith; by such methods will be advanced theology's prime concern with truth. Of professional theologians, Berger found most affinity with Wolfhart Pannenberg.

It is not necessary to endorse all Peter Berger's views to find his suggestions refreshing, not least because they come from a

ociologist of such high repute. Those who start from an
cceptance of God's self-disclosure can only learn with grati-
ude a way of looking at everyday behaviour which shows
nan pointing back to God in whose image he is made. It is
aluable both for confirming and for commending the faith.
His book warrants careful reading, but some sentences from the
concluding remarks' will convey its flavour.

A rediscovery of the supernatural will be, above all, a
regaining of openness in our perception of reality. It will not
only be, as theologians influenced by existentialism have
greatly overemphasized, an overcoming of tragedy. Perhaps
more importantly it will be an overcoming of triviality.
In openness to the signals of transcendence the true proportions of our experience are rediscovered. This is the comic
relief of redemption; it makes it possible for us to laugh and
to play with a new fullness. (p. 119)

uch an attitude in no way escapes the moral challenge of
umanity's predicament. On the contrary, it involves paying
1e most careful attention to human affairs, 'just because, in
1e words of a New Testament writer, it is in the midst of
1ese affairs that "some have entertained angels unawares"
Hebrews 13.2).' (p. 120)

4

Ve must attend to mysteries which lie beyond the limits of
veryday experience, aspects of existence which may be quite
idden to all scientific methods of investigation. We shall find
urselves covering ground which modern theologians com-
1only neglect. We shall ask and sometimes answer questions
'hich the learned often consider improper but which ordinary
1en or women, whose attitudes could be wiser than those of
1e learned, persist in asking. What am I; am I 'a free spirit,
reated with a view to eternal fellowship with a personal
'od,'[13] or am I merely the temporary product of impersonal
rces? Is the species to which I belong different in kind from
1e other species which inhabit the earth; or is the difference
1erely one of degree, we being the most advanced so far?

If the first alternative be true, must we then reckon with the 'existence' of some realm of the spirit not accessible to scientific investigation?

A positive answer to that question runs so strongly against current ways of thought that it takes an effort to realize that until a century ago hardly anyone would have considered answering it negatively.

Yet a positive answer has one immediate advantage. It ends mankind's embarrassing isolation. Without it the theologian must think of God as existing in solitary state, the only spiritual existent until, at the end of an unimaginably long process, an animal at last evolved to the point where a thin whisker of spirit reached uncertainly out towards the eternal Spirit, the Creator.

Traditional Christianity teaches something far different. The eternal God, who is Spirit, created first many spiritual beings having separate existence in dependence upon him. These were intelligences capable of choice (some of them rebelled, the origin of demons) but without material bodies, unrelated to any material creation, unbounded by the limitations of time or space; living in a universe so different from ours, that we can only speak of them in the language of analogy, never describe them as they are in themselves.

The word 'angel' is the English form of a Greek word meaning 'messenger', as does its Hebrew counterpart in the Old Testament. It was essentially as messengers from God that those visitors from another world were encountered by the ancient Hebrews. It is possible to trace a certain development in the way Israel understood angels during the thousand or so years represented in the Old Testament. The New Testament writers inherited a considerable tradition of how to interpret such visitations. It is significant both that angels were recognized in the earliest days of Christianity and that similar beings feature in other religions also.

The only way to say anything about angels is to invest them with some aspects of human experience. Their own mode of life, being in no way embodied, is so different from ours that we can only speak of it in negatives. They have to assume something like human form in order to make themselves known to us, but we should not suppose that even the least sentimental representation of an angel in art depicts anything more than the form assumed temporarily for the purpose of impinging on human senses. In themselves angels are pure spirit, no more corporeal than God himself.

Modern teachers sometimes present them as aspects of God, flashes of divine energy, claiming that their anthropomorphic representation in Scripture is due to the fear of blasphemy which prevented the biblical writers from describing God in human terms. Sometimes, indeed, God may have been his own messenger; each incident needs to be examined separately. But there is some danger in confusing angels with God. Angels, like God, are pure spirit; but they are not God, they are creatures, and to worship them would be no less idolatrous than to worship a fellow human being.

Demons should be taken seriously as fallen angels; that is, as spiritual created intelligences who have rebelled against their Creator. If they are regarded as personifications of evil, we gain some valuable insights into the nature of evil. It is negative, the denial of good. It is therefore secondary and derivative, not original, for it is the perversion of something that already exists. It is also ultimately self-frustrating, for it has cut itself off from the source of its own being and, like a cut flower, will eventually wither and die. But although it is thus ultimately futile, evil has still an appalling capability for harm.

It is doubtful whether an abstract interpretation of demons does justice either to Christian tradition or to human experience. It is often said that devil-possession was simply the way that in pre-scientific days people described the more spectacular effects of physical or mental illness. The Gospel accounts, however, distinguish carefully between healing the sick and casting out demons from the possessed. There is also a surprisingly consistent body of evidence down to our own days of human lives fouled up in ways not easily explained in medical or social terms.

It is reasonable, therefore, at least to consider the hypothesis of other modes of existence than our own, modes within the created order but unconnected with the material creation of which we are a part. We may think of a spiritual realm where unembodied intelligences can operate in some way analogously to our operations, though without the limitations imposed by time and space; a sphere of the creation where God's purposes are furthered, but where negative choice is tragically possible.

Once accept such a possibility and two problems instantly confront you: a suitable vocabulary for talking about such things and reliable criteria for deciding when you are dealing with phenomena which require supernatural description. In what follows I owe a great deal to the Symposium by members of the Fellowship of St Alban and St Sergius published under the title *The Angels of Light and the Powers of Darkness*,[14] and in particular to papers by Professor H. A. Hodges and Fr Gilbert Shaw.

Christian thinkers make a fundamental distinction between the uncreated and the created, between the Creator and everything else which in all its variety is included under the term creation. It is necessary, before proceeding further, to rid our minds of the pervasive modern notion that creation means only material creation.

The angels, though part of creation, are, writes Father Shaw, 'outside our material order and operate upon it from their own sphere.' Distinguishing between the angelic and the demonic sphere, he calls the former the 'spiritual sphere', 'that which is in the light of God receiving and reflecting the light of God.' The habitat of the demons he calls the 'sphere of fallen spirits', 'from which they endeavour—alas, all too often successfully— to penetrate into the material sphere which was created to render its glory of space and time and of the human free will to God who created it.'[15] Human beings, because of what they are, should have cognizance of both spheres, the material and the spiritual. Father Shaw gives an interesting account of the factors in our recent culture which have so reduced our openness to the spiritual; he reminds us that both angels and demons are to be clearly distinguished from disembodied human spirits.

'Do not neglect to show hospitality to strangers', warns the Letter to the Hebrews, 'for thereby some have entertained angels unawares.'[16] The discerning of angels (or demons) sounds an archaic enterprise, if not a little mad. But if it were more widely practised the world would be a wiser place. How does one become aware of an angel?

'Angels present a problem for the theory of knowledge', writes Professor Hodges, 'because in their proper being they are not perceptible by our senses.'[17] In that they are not unique. Our own minds or souls (of which more anon) are not perceptible by our senses; yet when we look at ourselves in a mirror we know that we are more than the body we see. Also we are aware that other people, like us, are more than what we see of them. They are human beings like us and will have at least some of the same reactions. But angels? They are quite alien. 'I suppose them to be like myself in the sense that they are conscious, intelligent, spiritual beings,' reflects Professor Hodges; 'but since their consciousness and intelligence must be very different from my own, my conception of them is therefore bound to be analogical and inexact ...'[18]

Hodges points out that our knowledge of angels rests basically on the authority of divine revelation. Without that authority the fleeting and ambiguous impressions of discarnate spiritual intelligences impinging on human life would not necessarily be interpreted as the Christian doctrine of angels. The interplay between the data of revelation and the philosophical, metaphysical constructions of theology provide a grid on which to interpret the fragmentary experience.

With this grid, we may assert with confidence that human nature includes a faculty of direct non-sensory perception; spirit, if you like, is capable of responding to spirit. Theology tells us that this faculty was impaired by the Fall and restored in Christ, though, as we know, it does not thrive in technological society. Direct perception through this faculty may trigger off our faculty for making images (imagination) so that we get a mental picture. If our imagination is well furnished with stereotypes, the spiritual perception will probably select a suitable one from those on hand in which to express itself. We may in consequence see what we believe to be a vision. But however vivid the image, it is not to be confused with the spiritual perception itself, to which it is merely the imaginative counterpart.[19] An angel, in fact, will look like your image of one.

The last point needs to be emphasized. Spiritual perception

is not the same thing as imagination. Imagination is the ability to make images. It is subjective, liable to be undisciplined, and has of itself no certain result in greater understanding or awareness. It is a good servant but a bad master, a tool which, however sharp, may be used badly or well. Spiritual perception, on the other hand, is the ability to perceive a presence in the spiritual sphere; that is, the ability to respond to a stimulus from outside.

Hodges points out that 'many in whom the power of direct spiritual perception is not developed' may yet have 'a kind of non-sensory awareness of an angelic presence on the "psychic" level';[20] the widespread experience of an atmosphere which triggers the imagination so that one seems aware of a clearly defined invisible presence. It is, sadly, often an evil-seeming presence; perhaps, the professor suggests, because the 'psychic' or lower levels of the self are more readily open to the fallen angels.

It is also possible to detect a spiritual presence—again, unfortunately, it is most commonly an evil presence—at work among particular groups of people. *Diabolos*, from which our word 'devil' comes, means 'a setter at variance'; and not infrequently we see relationships between people being 'bedevilled' in a manner for which there is no reasonable explanation, the people concerned behaving quite out of character. Hodges speaks of 'a planned campaign of disintegration'; the historian Gerald Bonner, in his book *The Warfare of Christ*, interpreted the 'court' of Hitler, and in particular the virtuous, domestic Himmler, in that light.[21]

Fortunately it is possible to be aware of spiritual presences of a good kind; to become aware of a shaft of holiness which pierces you and holds you transfixed, so different is it in quality from everyday experience. It is less easy to identify a particular type of good spiritual presence than it is an evil one. Angels, unlike demons, do not act for themselves; they are 'ministers of grace' who, as we shall see, attend the prayers of the faithful. We may cite two direct descriptions of spiritual experience, both of which have been enshrined in fine literature; though one at least is fictitious, it is not hard to believe that they derive ultimately from spiritual perception. Perhaps because

hey have been artistically turned, they may illuminate a
necessarily closely reasoned discussion.

The first is from T. S. Eliot's poem 'Little Gidding':

> If you came this way
> Taking any route, starting from anywhere,
> At any time or at any season,
> It would always be the same: you would have to put off
> Sense and notion. You are not here to verify,
> Instruct yourself, or inform curiosity
> Or carry report. You are here to kneel
> Where prayer has been valid. . . .[22]

The other example is from that most charming of children's
books, *The Wind in the Willows*. The Water Rat and the Mole
were out on the river at night, looking for the adventurous
young otter cub who was missing. Led by mysterious music
which ran through the river-noise, they came to an island.
This is the place of my song-dream, the place the music played
to me', whispered the Rat, as if in a trance. 'Here, in this holy
place, here, if anywhere, we shall find him.'

Then suddenly the Mole felt a great Awe fall upon him, an
awe that turned his muscles to water, bowed his head, and
rooted his feet to the ground. It was no panic terror—
indeed he felt wonderfully at peace and happy—but it was
an awe that smote and held him and, without seeing, he
knew it could only mean that some august Presence was very,
very near.[23]

Eventually they looked up and saw the Friend and Protector
of small animals playing on his pipes while the baby Otter
slept between his hooves. The Mole looked up.

And still as he looked, he lived; and still as he lived he
wondered.

'Rat!' he found breath to whisper, shaking. 'Are you
afraid?'

'Afraid?' murmured the Rat, his eyes shining with unutter-
able love. 'Afraid! Of *Him*? O, never, never! And yet—and
yet—O Mole, I am afraid!'

Then the two animals, crouching to the earth, bowed their heads and did worship.[24]

And the sun suddenly shone, its first rays dazzling them; and the Vision vanished from sight and memory.

5

We are dealing with a phenomenon sometimes described by the adjective 'numinous'. It was the German theologian Rudolf Otto who first brought the term into use, as a means of describing the experience of 'the Holy', especially in its immediate effect on those who encountered it.[25] The Rat's experience on the island might almost be a text-book illustration of what Otto means by the numinous as awareness of the Holy: *mysterium tremendum et fascinans*. The Rat is possessed simultaneously by love and fear.

Otto conducted his inquiry into the Holy by way of the non-rational or supra-rational elements in the nature of divinity. His approach was thus closer to that of the present book than is that of many writers who regard such phenomena as human reactions pure and simple, their origins rooted in factors to be investigated by psychology rather than theology. I wish, however, to go beyond Otto in stressing not the effect of these experiences, but their external causes.

The numinous occurs when something of the Creator's own energy makes itself felt within and flames out through the created order. Behind all the angels stands God their Lord, the Lord of hosts as the Hebrews rightly called him. The Lord who is Spirit stands behind every movement of spirit, and every movement of spirit is a response returned to the Lord; even that of the rebellious angels who in their total perversity still witness to their Creator.

The Lord is paramount. That is why all the traditions of mankind about the supreme power, however confused or mistaken, nevertheless have some kinship with him. He has created mankind in his own image, and that image is chiefly to be seen in the human spirit. There is no human being so depraved as to have lost totally the marks of that image. Christians are able, therefore, to assert dogmatically that in Christ God has revealed himself uniquely for the salvation of mankind; and also that God has not left himself without witness in other religions (or, presumably, in the smaller but steadily increasing number of those who have no religion at all). We are likely therefore to find similar attitudes of response to the divine both beyond the boundaries of Christian faith and within them.

The creation is vastly larger than we are able effectively to grasp. Talk of God tends to be cosy and parochial. But he is Lord of the great as well as of the small: Lord of the expanding universe and of any beyond it. The 'our' in the amazing and overworked phrase 'our Lord' is used with no exclusive overtone. Because we are so much the centre of our own world, we forget the relative youth of our species, of our planet, of our universe. It needs a mental revolution to convince us that the spiritual creation is vastly larger, more powerful, and more ancient (those space-time terms are used analogically) than the material. To us, 'visitors from another world' seem to be intruders threatening the closed securities of our finite, material world. In reality the position is reversed. We are the intruders, the latecomers, the few among the many.

We are none the less right to claim for ourselves an importance in the scheme of things quite disproportionate to human size. That importance is not to be deduced with any certainty from scientific observation. Apart from divine revelation it would only be a brave hope. It is due wholly to decisions taken in the divine inscrutability.

> I cannot tell why He, whom angels worship,
> Should set His love upon the sons of men....[26]

But the revelation of Christ insists that he did; and the Creator has taken unto himself a part of the creation which is not, like him, spirit, but includes perishable matter.

The discussion has now penetrated far behind the edges of mystery. In speaking of angels we concern ourselves with those bright spirits who wait on the central mystery itself, the eternal God who is beyond even the most exalted angelic creation, God in himself, the eternal life of Father, Son, and Spirit.

The mystery of human existence, the spiritual and the

animal, turns out to be *musterion* in the biblical sense of a secret in the process of being revealed. The task of theology confronted with the mystery of man is to see what God has made known, to arrange and to present as fittingly as may be the sense of that revelation so as to make it more possible for finite minds to grasp its essentials. Theology is effective when as a result of its deliverances human beings know that in the end they do not grasp the truth; they are grasped by it, they accept and adore.

We cannot stop short of that point if we are to know the truth about our species.

3

Adam From First To Last

O Lord, our Lord,
how majestic is thy name in all the earth!
....
When I look at thy heavens, the work of thy fingers,
   the moon and the stars which thou hast established;
what is man that thou art mindful of him,
   and the son of man that thou dost care for him?[1]

Hard-boiled moderns echo the Psalmist's question. It rings with notable absurdity in the theatre of the Absurd, and it is the main concern of the present chapter.

The Psalmist continues in words that have an obvious relation to the argument just propounded.

Yet thou hast made him little less than God,

                              [in A.V. 'the angels']
   and dost crown him with glory and honour.
Thou hast given him dominion over the works of thy hands;
   thou hast put all things under his feet,
all sheep and oxen,
   and also the beasts of the field,
the birds of the air, and the fish of the sea,
   whatever passes along the paths of the sea.[2]

We cannot escape the irony of the human situation. Mankind's God-given control over his environment has never been greater, indeed is advancing with ever-increasing speed; yet each new discovery or skill raises a fresh threat to human survival or underlines an existing one. Paradox appears at two levels. Politically (under which are included the social and economic) the problem is for the species to live together as a whole, in freedom and fairness. On the personal level the stubborn fact of death cuts down even the most brilliant and valuable individual, reducing all alike to a heap of decaying matter.

Christian teaching has something to say to the human predicament at both levels, but in point of fact the Church has seldom managed to present it satisfactorily.

Perhaps particularly in Protestant England, the emphasis has been too heavily moralistic. It has been assumed that the chief end of religion is to enable virtuous living. The Church of England, in its position of national Church, found itself cast in the role of moral schoolmaster or indeed policeman. Something of the sort is written into that Book of Common Prayer which until the last decade provided the ordinary Englishman's Christian formation.

> *Question.* What is thy duty towards thy neighbour?
> *Answer.* My duty towards my neighbour, is to love him as myself, and to do to all men, as I would they should do unto me: To love, honour and succour my father and mother: To honour and obey the King, and all that are put in authority under him: To submit myself towards all my governors, teachers, spiritual pastors and masters: To order myself lowly and reverently to all my betters: To hurt nobody by word or deed: To be true and just in all my dealings: To bear no malice or hatred in my heart: To keep my hands from picking and stealing, and my tongue from evil-speaking, lying and slandering: To keep my body in temperance, soberness and chastity: Not to covet nor desire other men's goods; but to learn and labour truly to get mine own living, and to do my duty in that state of life, unto which it shall please God to call me.[3]

Excellent teaching, giving detailed instruction in Christian behaviour; but it presupposes a stable community, solidly Christian to the point where citizenship and religious obedience are the two sides of a coin. The religious obedience is further defined by membership of the Established Church. Between the view of society which the Catechism assumes and the open, pluralistic society of today extends a long course of grudging modifications. England became a nation accepting 'broadly

Christian' values, as first Nonconformist Protestant bodies, then Roman Catholics, Jews, and eventually adherents of any faith or none, were admitted to full rights. Now, of course, even the 'broadest' Christian values do not pass unchallenged.

Part at least of the Established Church's failure to influence these developments more effectively has been the lack of an explicit theology. The criticism sometimes heard that the Church of England has no coherent theology is untrue. The Reformation took over the massive traditional structures of belief concerning God the Holy Trinity, and the two natures of Christ. So central, indeed, were these beliefs for those who shaped the English Reformation that, where most other declarations of faith drawn up by the Reformers start by defining the source of authority for belief (the Bible), the English Thirty-nine Articles of Religion begin by expounding the traditional belief in God.

The fundamental theology to be found in the Articles, however, is not argued there. It is assumed and stated. Furthermore, the Articles were never imposed upon the laity as their standard of belief. They were intended to regulate the teaching of the clergy and had certain similar functions in the universities. The standard for the laity was the Catechism, whose fundamental theology, though finely expressed, occupies but a small proportion of the total syllabus. In this connection, however, the liturgical worship of the Prayer Book is important; the layman who worshipped according to its rites Sunday after Sunday from childhood to old age could hardly avoid absorbing a great deal of solid theology even though he may not have assimilated it intellectually.

It was no doubt to the sermon that the layman looked for theological education if he desired it. The sermon was not perhaps at any time the best medium for the communication of subtle truth. If also the parson was not theologically minded, or considered the truths of divinity too strong for his people's stomach, those people never learned any. So the scene was set for the modern situation where 'theology' can be used as a term of contempt; it was contrasted with the 'practical' religion of sound morality.

The extent of impoverishment which the optional place of

theology in English religion brought did not appear until the present century. It was when the gap widened startlingly between the moral standards acceptable in society at large and the moral standards of the Church that the divorce between theological conviction and religious practice was seen to be serious. Historians may well look back to the period between the two World Wars as the watershed, and perhaps to no more painful a moment than the crisis over the King's abdication in 1936.

The novelist and playwright Charles Morgan, who lived through that period, illuminated it with some perceptive comment. He reflected upon his own position as a member of the Church of England who rarely attended church though he valued the institution and its priests. Musing on 'The Empty Pews', including his own, he asked why the Church had 'gone dead' on so many of his contemporaries. In part it was due to a change in social habit since Victorian days.

> Some were drawn to church by a profound and lively religious conviction; others by a religious habit of mind which, though often vague and touched by scepticism, prevailed upon conduct; and many more, who gave little or no thought to religion from Monday to Saturday, went to church on Sunday in obedience to social custom.[4]

The first group, he believed, were no fewer than before. The second group were less likely to come to church since they were likely to refer their behaviour to a social than to a religious conscience. The third group, in Victorian times the largest, had by 1945 virtually disappeared.

Thirty years later Morgan's analysis still stands, although during those years the morality of those who base it on social norms has diverged even further from that which is referred directly to Christian belief. His comments on the steps commonly taken by the clergy to halt the drift from their churches are even more apt since the coming of secular Christianity than they were before. 'Some priests', he remarks, 'try to make their sermons more interesting by preaching, as they say, "topically".'[5] The adverb today would be 'relevantly'.

They seem, when they mount the pulpit, deliberately to put off from them the authority of their calling. They are so anxious not to appear parsonical that they avoid even a deliberately Christian approach to their subject, and discuss it as if they were leader-writers or politicians or merchants.[6]

Morgan found that such hesitancy repelled more than it attracted. The parson might be 'very human', but he was not much help.

A hesitant layman will never be held by a preacher who plays down to him.... If a preacher's argument ... is in effect a lay argument of the kind that may be heard in any club or read in any newspaper, then, whether his discourse be wise or unwise, he is teaching what men do not go to church to learn.[7]

Charles Morgan was equally interesting in his assessment of what people who go to church wanted to hear: the subject under discussion, whatever it might be, referred to 'the inmost truths of Christianity'[8]. His plea was for the Church boldly 'to resume her splendours of the mind and spirit', if necessary working hard to find suitable parables. He dropped a broad hint that the Roman Catholic Church, undergirded by prayer from its monks and nuns, had the edge over the Church of England. Contemplation, he believed, was more important than social endeavour.

The past thirty years have thrown into relief another area where the Roman Catholic Church may have the edge over the Church of England: that of clear and intelligible moral teaching. Anglican polemics have made much of our tradition of treating lay people as responsible adults. We do not lay down hard rules which people must obey on pain of sanctions. Our method is to indicate broad standards, to isolate general principles, but to leave detailed decisions to the educated and enlightened conscience of church members.

In our own day the contrast with Roman Catholic methods has been in the sphere of sexual morality. Where Anglican moral theologians refer a question such as artificial contraception to the several factors involved, leaving the concerned

27

Christian to grade the priority of those matters according to his own conviction, the Roman Catholic Church lays down an absolute principle, indicates precisely the attitudes and conduct which conform to that principle and those which subvert it—and provides a discipline of forgiveness and restoration for those who accept the principle but fail to live up to it.

The widening rift between traditional Christian standards and those which are socially acceptable has put the Anglican method at a new disadvantage. Christians are as subject to the pressures of the society they live in as anyone else. If they never hear the traditional teaching except when it is caricatured they will grow up, unlike their predecessors, without that element in the infra-structure of their attitudes; and they may assume that time has made ancient good uncouth when it is simply that the traditions have fallen into disuse.

Intimate relations between the sexes outside marriage, for instance, were discouraged by the twin fears of pregnancy and of venereal disease. Medical advances are such that with the proper precautions neither event need occur (the fact that precautions are so often not taken does not affect the present argument). Is it therefore in order for a man and a woman to come together intimately, with their eyes open, aware that their commitment to each other is strictly limited to the giving and receiving of pleasure without aftermath or recrimination. Many serious elements in present-day culture would favour the idea, and on a humanistic assessment of the factors, it is hard to disagree.

Christians and humanists have lately found a language which expresses in this field their shared concerns. They contrast the genuinely personal relationship of giving and receiving with the depersonalizing effect of exploitation. They insist that respect for persons is the first good, that rules are tools to encourage such respect or to limit its abuse; and 'good' which such rules may express is determined by the particular circumstances. Christians are thus found treating as open questions matters which their forbears had always decided one way. When they wish to say that changing marriage partners is wrong, they do so on the grounds of its effects on the children. They will weigh up each case separately and believe that whatever is done finally with a good conscience is right.

What is missing, of course, is the note of absolute certainty: 'Thus saith the Lord.' A thing is right or wrong. Here the dogmatist, be he Catholic, Protestant, or, for that matter, Marxist, is at a great advantage. For he can say that a matter which is in itself wrong may, in certain circumstances, be the lesser evil. And if men or women are trapped in a situation of wrong too strong for them to break out of it, the Catholic system of penance provides a way of freeing them which does not involve any 'merciful lie' of saying that black is white.

There can be no doubt that the rapidly developing human ability to control our environment causes confusion. Often the old norms of conduct no longer match the confronting options. Two basic alternatives exist for tackling such a situation. You can formulate a new set of norms derived from the new circumstances. Or you can dig deeply into the received norms, discovering their essential thrust and trying to engage it into the new situation. The second discipline is the theologian's way. It is hard, and could not be undertaken without the help of the Holy Spirit. It is the only way to save Christianity from a slide into endless relativism.

In current discussions of sexual relations, therefore, we should rejoice in the widespread emphasis on respect for personality. But we must insist on a Christian, theological definition of personality and personal fulfilment, and should not hide from our humanist fellow-travellers that certain courses of conduct may in themselves be intrinsically wrong. Failure to be clear over such matters may result in smoother relationships immediately, but in the long run it means the betrayal of what we stand for. A Christian opinion which has lost its distinctiveness is like salt that has lost its savour.

2

In no other area of experience has the Church's reticence in teaching theology proved more unfortunate than in the field of understanding what it means to be human. Others have come in to fill the gap, Marx and Freud their founding fathers; and Christian thinkers have too often felt obliged to bow to their authority, a very different matter from profiting from some of their insights.

Let us make clear what we mean. The essential for any theological interpretation is that it relates whatever it is interpreting to what is known of God; or, in Charles Morgan's phrase, to 'the inmost truths of Christianity'. An interpretation which falls short of the theological is basically humanist. It is important to realize also that 'humanist' does not necessarily imply an atheistic bias. A humanistic analysis will often be the most appropriate one; only if it proceeds from a closed humanism will it be anti-theological.

Fortunately there is a long tradition in Anglican theology for a framework of ultimate relationships with the divine into which the observations of social science may be inserted. The work of nineteenth-century theologians, notably F. D. Maurice and B. F. Westcott, has stimulated modern approaches which have been greatly helped by trends within Old Testament scholarship.[9]

There have been problems of adjustment, 'demarcation disputes' between the several academic disciplines concerned with understanding the human phenomenon, which are still unresolved. The sciences which describe human behaviour were late arrivals in the learned world and had considerable trouble in distinguishing their particular concerns and techniques from those of the historian, economist, moralist, and theologian. The result can be confusing for the reader who wishes to see how the description of man in one discipline compares with that in the others.

For some time now theologians have been using some of the insights of anthropologists and social psychologists to interpret the Old Testament understandings of man. Perhaps surprisingly, those ancient ways of understanding human society and behaviour can be enlightening even today, especially in the vexed relationship between individual and corporate aspects.

Old Testament scholarship distinguishes between several sources which underlie the early chapters of Genesis, where so much of the basic Hebrew understanding of man is concentrated. The first big change occurs in chapter 2, in the middle of verse 4, where 'the second account of creation' is held to begin. To a certain type of modern mind the account of the Lord God's activities which follows is naive, childish, and unworthy of serious consideration: 'anthropomorphic' is the favourite word of dismissal. And so it is, if you take it to be a straight attempt to describe what actually happened.

It seems surprising, however, that it was ever taken in that way. Clearly it was not so when it was written into its present form. We should think of ancient tales told and retold in the tents of Israel, and at the ancient holy places in the land. At some relatively late point in the history of those tales, someone wrote them down, combining variant 'traditions' which had been handed down in widely separated places. Whoever did this was most skilful and sophisticated, so that it is absurd to think that he would have been less able than we are to spot the join or to see the conflicting order of events in the two accounts of creation.

The fact that the compiler made no attempt to reconcile the two accounts, smoothly though he arranged their literary join, should make us more careful to see what he was trying to do. Presumably he was not seeking to produce a would-be scientific, chronological account of the creation. Even if the material was originally just that, it has emerged from the compiler's hand as something different.

Genesis 1 contains an account of creation with all the emphasis on God the Creator. Majestic language conveys an exalted understanding of God the one Creator and Ruler of everything that was known in the ancient world. Scholars point to other parts of the Bible which speak in similar vein, notably the prophecy of Ezekiel, and connect the account with the exile in Babylon, a city which included in its own heritage an 'epic of creation' in some respects like Genesis 1.

The version which begins at Genesis 2.4 is far less majestic and indeed more domestic in feel. The Lord God (different words for the Deity are the chief clues in distinguishing sources) 'formed man of dust from the ground' before there was any vegetable life or even rain. Then he planted a garden (Eden) and put the man in it. He then produced trees, including the mysterious ones of life and the knowledge of good and evil. (A piece of archaic geography based on four rivers interrupts the action.) Then the Lord God tells the man to till the garden. He may help himself to the fruit of every tree except that of the knowledge of good and evil (the tree of life is not mentioned). The Lord God then addresses himself to the problem of the man's solitude. He formed all manner of birds and beasts out of the ground, and brought them to the man to see what he would call them; but none of them was a helper fit for him.

> So the LORD God caused a deep sleep to fall upon the man, and while he slept took one of his ribs and closed up the place with flesh; and the rib which the LORD God had taken from the man he made into a woman and brought her to the man. Then the man said,
> > 'This at last is bone of my bones
> > and flesh of my flesh;
> > she shall be called Woman,
> > because she was taken out of Man.'
> Therefore a man leaves his father and his mother and cleaves to his wife, and they become one flesh. And the man and his wife were both naked, and were not ashamed.[10]

Those words clearly go back to a primitive stage in human culture. They are about an experience which belongs to the irreducible bedrock of human existence. Men and women are different, but when compared with any other species they belong together. The particular tradition of human experience which formulated the answer of Genesis to the question is clearly man-centred, but the difference between the sexes is nothing by comparison with their unity over against any other species.

Moreover, the human species is in a position to dominate the animal world. All other species were brought to him to be named; and in the ancient belief, to know the name of something, let alone to bestow the name, is to have power over it.

Man, then, is in control. But man himself is a creature. The Lord God made him out of the dust of the ground in the same way as he made all the other creatures. When a man dies, his body disintegrates like any other animal body. But the Lord God had breathed into his nostrils that which made him a living being. (Additional evidence of the incident's long history before being given its final setting comes from the fact that the word for 'living being' would logically have applied to the animals too, though it is not so used.)

The man is not simply a creature whom the Lord God made; he is one whom the Lord God addresses, telling him what he may and may not do. He is a creature whose 'addressability' marks him off from the beasts. He can understand.

He can also respond, which involves him at once in the power of choice. The last phrase of our quotation is poignant— 'and the man and his wife were both naked and were not ashamed.' Genesis 2 looks back to a vanished state, a state that was already long vanished when the tale behind the text was first told. Even then nakedness was a cause of shame. We can see Paradise only through the distorting lens of Paradise lost.

Chapter 3, which tells us how Paradise was lost, is so well known (and regularly taught) that we need call attention to a few dominant points only. But the whole chapter repays close attention. It uses ancient tales to make sense of human experience which for all its glory falls so very far short of what it might be.

The nakedness at the end of chapter 2 is symbolic. Straightforward enjoyment of human bodies is no longer possible. Natural innocence has vanished and has left instead embarrassment. A naked person is unprotected, at a disadvantage, as modern 'interrogators' know so well. That is not the case with animals. It is a distinctive mark of being human, a sign that we have exchanged innocence for something else. The Lord God in his mercy takes it seriously, himself making for Adam and his wife garments of skins. Some Christian commentators have seen here a first intimation of the sacrifice which God provided for human salvation.

Genesis 3, like Genesis 2, is a panel of ancient cartoons arranged to answer primary questions: Why is life like this? The terms of the punishments which the Lord God inflicts are revealing. Why do snakes arouse such revulsion that most people's instinctive reaction is to kill them? Why is childbirth, most fulfilling of female functions, marred by pain and danger? Why does male domination so often make a mockery of companionship in marriage? Why is physical labour a struggle and a blight as well as a creative joy? Each of these matters shows how far the promise of chapter 2 has been marred in its fulfilment.

Let us finally consider the figure of the Lord God. He, like God in chapter 1, is the transcendent Creator, but he is much more involved in his creation. He 'walks in the garden in the cool of the day;' a charming phrase which may suggest naive anthropomorphism to the sophisticated but which in the context is so much more effectively read as the reflection of an encounter with the *mysterium tremendum et fascinans*. Somewhere along the line of the story's transmission, someone had known at first hand the terror of the Lord:

> Whither shall I go from thy Spirit?
>> Or whither shall I flee from thy presence?
> If I ascend to heaven, thou art there!
>> If I make my bed in Sheol, thou art there!
> If I take the wings of the morning
>> and dwell in the uttermost parts of the sea,
> even there thy hand shall lead me,
>> and thy right hand shall hold me.[11].

In the setting of such primary relationships it is useful to consider how 'the man' becomes 'Adam', a proper name. Readers in the habit of comparing different English versions may have noticed that in the Authorized Version 'the man' becomes 'Adam' in 2.19; but in the Revised Standard Version the personal name does not appear until 3.17. In fact, of course, 'man' and 'Adam' are the same word in the original Hebrew. It is, however, perfectly proper to call Adam 'the man' throughout the chapter. Adam, it is often said, is everyman and Adam's story is every man's story. 'Mankind' is the block from which the individual human being is a chip. The relation of the individual to the totality of mankind will occupy our attention later. For the moment we may say that there are marked differences between the biblical understanding of that relationship and the understanding of much Christian thought.

3

Most of the events described in Genesis chapters 4 to 11 are told in the same accents we have found in chapters 2 and 3. Chapter 2, we may say, describes the human condition ideally, as it was meant to be: slung between the Lord God and the beasts, in healthy relations with both. Chapter 3 describes the condition which has developed, one of revolt against the Lord God and of being at odds within the species and with the environment. With Genesis 4 begins a sort of pre-history. Cain and Abel show the primal antagonism between nomad shepherd and peasant farmer. The first murder is a fratricide; and the Lord God steps in, as he did in the matter of nakedness, to retrieve the situation. The 'mark of Cain', contrary to popular belief, is a protection. Appalling though his crime, this man is not to be considered outside the law, for he is still within the human community.

And it is a single community. At the end of chapter 4, the Genesis writer picks up the first faint echoes of remotest history, for Cain's descendants and those of Adam's third son, Seth, preserve the names of ancient tribes; and they are all related. The proto-world of Genesis included no good old days. It was an evil world and was brought to an end with Noah's flood. But before that two obscure incidents show how delicate was mankind's place in the world. 'The sons of God saw that the daughters of men were fair', which refers perhaps to seduction by fallen angels; and 'the Nephilim were on the earth'—giants perhaps, just possibly the memory of some non-Adamic race of near-men.[12]

The story of Noah's flood describes a disaster by immersion repeated in such diverse human cultures that it seems best to connect it with historical memory however attenuated. Details in the alleged descent of all later mankind from one or other of Noah's sons have been made the basis of all manner of racial discrimination; surprisingly, since the narrative shows quite clearly that the difference between the races is superficial compared with their unity.[13] It is, incidentally, interesting that the Israelites with all their awareness of being separated as the

Chosen People still kept among their traditions the memory of an ancestry shared with their later enemies.

Chapter 11 ends the universal proto-history of Genesis; for the next chapter introduces Abraham, and with him starts the saga of Israel. The final episode from most ancient times is that of the Tower of Babel. It reaffirms all the main lines of the understanding of man which we have just seen unfolded. The men of Babel decided to build a tower which should reach to heaven, so as to prevent any further interference from the Lord. And the Lord came down and scattered them so that they lost touch with each other. Out of touch, their languages separated so that they could no longer understand each other.

Here an ancient memory of some great building long since in ruins forms the subject of a cartoon to answer the question: Why, since we are all one species, can we not all understand one another's speech? The resulting myth was used in the compilation of Genesis in order to reinforce a basic lesson. Man is neither God nor a beast, but has a place in the scheme of things slung between the two. Human self-sufficiency, the attempt to dispense with God, is doomed to failure. Man is not finally autonomous, and to act as if he is will bring confusion. The setting is primitive; the message has never been more topical than it is today.

The human race is a unity bound together in a kinship deeper than any diversity. That unity and its constituent members was designed to exist at its own level: neither a disembodied spirit like an angel, nor a spiritless body like a beast. The very simplicity of the cartoons in which Genesis presents these fundamental proportions of human life makes their basic humanity relevant at every level of cultural sophistication.

The matter of the individual's relation to the community is too complicated to be expressed in cartoon form. For the earlier part of Israel's history, more weight seems to have been put on the people as a whole than on the individuals composing it; indeed, it is by no means clear whether the accounts of Abraham, Isaac, and Jacob record the wanderings of individuals or of tribes. Some of what seems to be the harsher legislation in the Books of the Law looks differently when you realize that an Israelite could only fulfil his potential within the nation which gave him significance. The well-being of the nation might have to take preference over that of the individual. Not until the exile in Babylon many hundreds of years after Moses did it become clear that 'the soul that sinneth, it shall die'. The force of the old saying 'the fathers have eaten sour grapes and the children's teeth are set on edge' was weakened.

Biblical scholars steeped in the late nineteenth-century liberal idealism hailed the emergence of individual responsibility in Hebrew life as liberation, a great advance from the primitive. Today, aware as we are of all the interlocking forces binding together human beings psychically, socially, and economically, we are less sure that growth away from solidarity was necessarily growth into maturity. The older sense of what it meant to be human contained its own validity.

That sense is more deeply present in the New Testament writings than a previous generation realized. One of the problems in the scientific study of the Bible has been to realize the extent to which the scholar's own presuppositions belonged to a tradition of thought running from the Renaissance through the (German) Enlightenment to nineteenth-century liberalism; cardinal among its assumptions was the autonomy of the individual.

More recent experience has challenged the assumption that the individual's emancipation from the community is the key to human progress. New Testament scholars tend to share the prevailing climate of opinion which prefers 'personality' to 'individual' and recognizes how greatly environmental and social factors influence personal development. They are more willing than were their predecessors, therefore, to take seriously 'semitic concepts' when they find them in the New Testament.

So widespread is the belief that an individual's vitality comes from the community to which he belongs that it may be thought of as part of the 'infra-structure of New Testament thought'; that is to say, it was so obvious to all concerned at the time that no one bothered to explain it. But it does break surface explicitly at certain points. A close look at one or two of them will advance the present discussion.

The first point is the manner in which Jesus is shown among

his disciples. Perhaps the most celebrated passage is the opening of the Sermon on the Mount.

> Seeing the crowds, he went up on the mountain, and when he sat down his disciples came to him. And he opened his mouth and taught them, saying: Blessed are . . .[14]

The solemnity of the occasion is obvious. The Master is, as it were, seated in his teaching chair to deliver words of no common authority. But who are his hearers? The crowds, who would have a better chance of hearing the words if the speaker was raised on an eminence, or the disciples gathered at his feet?

Fortunately Matthew's Gospel is so clearly contrived in its presentation that we can deduce his general principles. Jesus is teaching specifically those who have enrolled with him in the school of the Kingdom of Heaven. His words are thus addressed in the first instance to the disciples. But the care taken to let the crowd also hear the words shows that 'the disciples' were not an exclusive group. Anyone prepared to find his blessedness where Jesus did was free to join.

Nevertheless, there was a nucleus. Matthew, Mark, and Luke all record Jesus's choice of twelve disciples; John does not give the complete list but refers to 'the twelve'.[15] In one way or another it is made clear that the number twelve has significance. The twelve 'special' disciples correspond to the twelve patriarchs, for they are the founding generation of a renewed Israel. The Twelve—it is St Luke particularly who makes clear the distinction—are also apostles, for they are sent forth to the nations to proclaim that the 'light for revelation to the Gentiles' has come;[16] the glory is that of Israel but is not to be confined there. The circle of the Twelve, broken by the defection of Judas, was mended by the election of Matthias.[17]

The circle of the Twelve by itself was empty. It was Jesus, around whom they gathered, who gave them their significance. Book after book has been written in our century to show in what ways he summed up and fulfilled the hopes of ancient Israel; notably the senses in which he accepted, rejected, or was designated Messiah, Son of David, Son of man. Suffice it to say that those titles were not precise terms to start with, though some of them had acquired fixed meanings among particular groups of Jews at that time, so that Jesus had to dissociate himself from them. We may say also that in so far as Jesus gave substance to these ancient shadows he did so actively and creatively, so that where he adopted them he altered them. There is no need to suppose that all the New Testament writers understood the terms, or the sense in which Jesus fulfilled them, in the same way.

One of the figures most often applied to Jesus, 'Son of man', had about it the suggestion that it was a corporate as well as an individual figure, rather in the same way that 'Israel' signifies both one of the patriarchs and the nation which claimed descent from him. There are occasions when 'Son of man' almost seems to stand for 'Jesus with his people around him'. Thus

> Jesus said to them, 'Truly, I say to you, in the new world, when the Son of man shall sit on his glorious throne, you who have followed me will also sit on twelve thrones, judging the twelve tribes of Israel.'[18]

St Luke records it rather differently:

> 'You are those who have continued with me in my trials; and I assign to you, as my Father assigned to me, a kingdom, that you may eat and drink at my table in my kingdom, and sit on thrones judging the twelve tribes of Israel.'[19]

The people of Jesus have a particular identity (and a particular destiny) which they share with each other by virtue of the relationship which they all enjoy with Jesus. He who sits at the centre of the circle shares his life to make a new corporate personality.

St Paul takes this up in his letters and defines it in terms of a new human solidarity. The effects of history have unfortunately masked the element of 'being called out' which is so prominent in the original understanding of 'church', so that to say, quite correctly, that St Paul elaborated the doctrine of the Church is to risk misunderstanding. St Paul discerns a new human solidarity so radical and far-reaching that 'in Christ' may be contrasted with 'in Adam'.[20]

We are concerned less with St Paul's theology than with the general sweep of the great vision of humanity renewed which he shared with the primitive Church in all its diversity of thought. That vision gave a distinctive perspective on human interrelationships which we may see dramatically in an episode from the Acts of the Apostles.

> But Saul, still breathing threats and murder against the disciples of the Lord, went to the high priest and asked him for letters to the synagogues at Damascus, so that if he found any belonging to the Way, men or women, he might bring them bound to Jerusalem. Now as he journeyed he approached Damascus, and suddenly a light from heaven flashed about him. And he fell to the ground and heard a voice saying to him, 'Saul, Saul, why do you persecute me?' And he said, 'Who are you, Lord?' And he said, 'I am Jesus whom you are persecuting ...'[21]

Saul had believed himself to be hunting down a group of dangerously deceived and deceiving fanatics. He found himself being addressed by their recently executed ring-leader. It would never again be possible for him to look upon a group of Christians except as a circle with Christ in the middle. Saul the persecutor had been brought face to face with the conviction which others had reached more gradually. All his later work for the Church as Paul the Apostle reflects his awareness of the Lord's continuing presence.

Life as the earliest Christians understood it was lived in two worlds at once. The old life, the solidarity of mankind 'in Adam', was the realm of commerce and politics and the family. It was not expected to last. The new life which had begun already to replace it was the solidarity of life 'in Christ' who was at present with them in hidden form only, a secret hidden from all but the chosen. Shortly it would be made open and public, when he would return and reign, and history, which meant mankind 'in Adam', would come to its final judgement and stop. In the meantime, he was present to them 'in the Spirit' and they shared in his life which had conquered death.

Two matters in the early Christian experience need further

attention now: the problem of time and the place of the Spirit.

The early Christians shared the Jewish understanding of time. It belonged to history, the unrolling of events in a sequence that would reach a climax when God intervened, suspended ordinary political government, and ruled directly through his chosen instrument. The Christians differed from their fellow Jews in having identified that instrument with Jesus. A battle had been fought (its climax at Calvary) in which the powers of this world, assisted by supra-human forces, had tried to prevent the start of God's direct rule. The attack had apparently succeeded, only to have its triumph reversed when God raised him from the dead. Mankind was now suspended in a pause until the Kingdom of God should be declared openly and unmistakably. During that pause the Church's task was to preach the gospel to all mankind, inviting all who would to enter the Kingdom while there was still time for choice.

Modifications of this scheme can be picked out in the New Testament writings, brought about by the increasing length of the pause. The Open Presence was at first expected very soon. There was no question of mankind continuing beyond that generation, so marriage, for instance, had no long-term importance;[22] nor had slavery.[23] At first St Paul had to reassure people that those who had died during the pause would not be at a disadvantage.[24] We see him coming to terms with the possibility of his own death[25] and, in the weariness of his imprisonment, beginning to long for it.[26] The letters to the Colossians and Ephesians, written in captivity, as well as 1 Peter, show that a code for Christian family life was developed, which must have grown in importance as the pause lengthened; there is also a rudimentary code of practice for Christians living in secular society.[27]

The Second Epistle of St Peter is often held to be a late work (and nothing to do with the Apostle) because it takes seriously the possibility of an indefinite delay in Christ's open return.

But do not ignore this one fact, beloved, that with the Lord one day is as a thousand years, and a thousand years as one day. The Lord is not slow about his promise as some count slowness, but is forbearing toward you, not wishing that any should perish, but that all should reach repentance. But the day of the Lord will come like a thief, and then the heavens will pass away with a loud noise, and the elements will be dissolved with fire, and the earth and the works that are upon it will be burned up.[28]

Other New Testament writings show varying adjustments to the problem of the delay.

Matthew, for instance, emphasizes church discipline, which seems more appropriate if the people of Jesus are to become an institution operating within human history. They are no casual group drawn together by a common enthusiasm, but a body which expresses the immediate authority of Jesus.

Truly, I say to you, whatever you bind on earth shall be bound in heaven, and whatever you loose on earth shall be loosed in heaven. Again I say to you, if two of you agree on earth about anything they ask, it will be done for them by my Father in heaven. For where two or three are gathered in my name, there am I in the midst of them.[29]

St Paul's experience on the way to Damascus, however, makes it clear that the Lord's presence in the Church is not to be dismissed as a means of explaining the long delay in his public return.

It was St Luke (taking him to be the author of the third Gospel and the Acts of the Apostles) who worked out most thoroughly the problem of continuing history. It is to him that we owe the timetable from Good Friday to Whitsun which is reflected in the Christian calendar. Thus the resurrection was followed by a period of forty days[30] before the event which rounded off the earthly work of Jesus, the ascension. Immediately before that event, Jesus told his disciples not to bother about the times of the Kingdom, but to bear their witness to him.[31] There followed a period of waiting in Jerusalem, during which the little company of 120 or so people elected a replacement for the traitor Judas. Then, at Pentecost, the Spirit came upon those who were faithfully waiting and, as with the firing of a starting-gun, the Church was launched on its world-wide mission.

The Fourth Gospel shows quite another way of handling the problem. Where Luke marshalls events in chronological sequence, John so deploys them as to bring out the simultaneity (or timelessness) of their deeper meaning; for though they are human, the events are the actions of God wrought out in human life, and so their proper reference is beyond time as much as within it. Pentecost, the coming of the Spirit, is thus divided between the cross and the resurrection. The Church is launched when Jesus commits his mother and the disciple whom he loved to each other's care.[32] The disciples received the Holy Spirit on the evening of Easter itself, and with it their commission as apostles ('sent') and the authorization to forgive or retain sins.[33] There is no ascension, but the death on the cross was a 'lifting up'[34] and marked the accomplishment of his work.[35] The simultaneity of all God's saving work through Christ is shown in many of the sayings of Jesus, not least in those that come from the earlier periods of his ministry:

He who hears my words and believes him who sent me, has eternal life; he does not come into judgment, but has passed from death to life.[36]

In fact both models, the 'sequential' and the 'simultaneous', are needed to minimize the injustice done to events which move both in time and beyond it.

The place of the Spirit in the making of the new human solidarity in Christ needs careful thought. Some of the early Christian Fathers were to divide human history into three periods. The period of God the Father coincided with that of the Old Testament. The period of God the Son covered the earthly life of Jesus. The period of the Holy Spirit began at Pentecost and still continues. Such schematization is exaggerated and misleading unless carefully qualified; neither the Father nor the Son nor the Spirit operates to the exclusion of the other Persons of the Blessed Trinity. It is, however, valuable to stress how mankind's links with God through Christ are maintained through the power of the Holy Spirit. Human solidarity in Christ, in short, is essentially a solidarity in the Spirit.

4

A theological approach to mankind thought of as a solidarity will be concerned with questions of history and its meaning. If those concerns be the long threads in a piece of woven cloth, the cross-threads will be about individual human destiny.

Present-day theologians are often unwilling to answer questions about individual survival after death, on the grounds that the biblical writings do not answer them. Under pressure, many of them will say that notions tending towards the immortality of the soul are alien to the genius of Hebrew religion, and so of the Christian when it is true to its roots. The Hebrew did not think of an embodied soul which could continue in a disembodied existence, but of an ensouled body. When, therefore, an Old Testament Hebrew spoke of a life after this one—which he did but seldom—he had in mind not the immortality of the soul but the resurrection of the body. Without such resurrection the unbodied soul continued at best a shadowy half-life. As for the few passages which suggested a genuine life for the disembodied spirit, they were either misunderstood or were the result of contamination by Greek culture.

A sharp distinction between Greek and Hebrew attitudes has been a mark notably of scholars of Reformed (Calvinist) or Lutheran persuasion. Catholic scholars are less disposed to find a conflict. Since one of the difficulties in biblical scholarship has been to avoid reading into the text the scholar's own presuppositions—a particularly complex matter when those presuppositions themselves are ultimately derived from the Bible—the recent growth of inter-confessional study is specially welcome.

Interconfessional agreement upon the social aspects of mankind is far easier to reach than it is upon the issues of personal destiny. Ancient battles have left the landscape deeply scarred: the old Reformation and Counter-Reformation issues of purgatory, indulgences, prayers for the dead, and the like. A more recent factor inhibiting Evangelical contributions to the matter is the fear of spiritualism, which threatens to raise uncontrollable and probably harmful influences. There is also a running dispute among Evangelical students of the Bible over whether the faithful departed are 'with Christ' in an active sense, or whether they are 'sleeping' until the general resurrection at the Lord's return.

The last matter may be dismissed briefly. David Winter, an Evangelical layman whose experience in journalism and broadcasting has taught him to wear his learning lightly, declares roundly: 'All such argument seems to me totally irrelevant.'[37] Time and space, he insists, are equally meaningless; for eternal life is a relationship with God through faith in Jesus Christ which begins here and now. Death, however traumatic, is to the person dying but an incident. 'Death is not the final enemy of man,' concludes Mr Winter. 'That is evil. Death is the final enemy of man's final enemy. Beyond it lies a new kind of life, where evil has no place at all.'[38]

But what kind of life? Clearly one in which personality and consciousness continue. Can we be more specific?

We have seen that traditional Christianity assumes the existence of a spiritual realm which is not under normal conditions directly accessible to our senses. Professor Hodges, discussing the problems (by no means insuperable) which the existence of a spiritual realm holds for the theory of knowledge, insists that ultimately we believe in it because it has been revealed to us.[39] Mr Winter would not disagree, but he indicates a bridge between ordinary ways of speech and the traditional teaching. It lies in the common notion and experience of 'personality'.

> The *real* John Jones—the thing that distinguishes him from Robert Brown, the distinctively personal 'him'—cannot die and does not die.[40]

Winter is careful to avoid saying that the soul is in the body like 'the ghost in the human machine';[41] the whole human being is a personality in bodily form, but that bodily form is not the personality.

True, John Jones has fair hair and blue eyes—but look at that verb! He 'has' them. They belong to him. But they, and all the other parts of his physical body, do not add up to a person. We should never describe his 'personality' in those terms. The real John Jones, the one who loves his wife and enjoys sunsets and growing roses, is much more than a computer linked to a machine. He is a person, and that is another way of saying that he is a 'soul'. And it is the *person* of John Jones that survives his death, not as a fleeting spirit or emanation, but as a man.[42]

If you believe that 'mind' uses brain (rather than that brain is 'mind'), then it is reasonable to suppose that, provided it can find another 'vehicle' for its activity, 'mind' can survive the death of the brain. 'Personality' clearly has more to do with 'mind' than with body; and if 'mind' can survive death, why not 'personality' as a whole? Winter favours a suggestion of D. M. Mackay,[43] Professor of Communications at Keele University, that personality is like a message. Our present bodies are a means of transmitting that message. In the life beyond, the same message will be transmitted through a new and better transmitter, of a totally different kind. That, Winter and Mackay believe, is in line with what St Paul teaches about a 'spiritual body'.[44]

'So where have we arrived?' We may answer Mr Winter's question in his own words before continuing the discussion along other lines.

When I die, my body disintegrates, but my personality—the 'real' me—lives on; this personality is going to express itself in the 'life beyond' in a totally different kind of body.[45]

So far so good. But if we are to consider the type of relationship which human beings in this life may enjoy with other spiritual beings, we must inquire more closely into how the 'real me' is made up.

It will help at this point to introduce the traditional three-fold analysis of man into body, soul, and spirit, and to clarify the relation between the last two and show how each of them bears on the concept of mind. 'Body' means 'that which is studied in anatomy and physiology, the physical organism which is born and dies, whose extension is confined within a few square feet of space and whose duration can be measured by a clock'.[46] But as well as his corporeal life a human being has a 'mental' life. It is this mental life which is best considered in two parts, a higher and a lower.

The lower part may be called 'soulish' from the Greek word *psyche*. Animals share at least part of the soulish life, with their awareness of sensation. But we experience sensations like hot and cold rather differently from the animals, for our higher mental life is able to interpret them in various ways. So, too, writes Father Shaw:

> The bodily appetites which we share with the beasts, such as hunger or sex, are different in us from what they are in them, because the higher level of our life informs the lower, the spirit illuminates or governs the soul.[47]

Most of this soul-life, being so closely bound to sensations received through the body, could hardly survive the body's death, except in the memory. Investigations have tended to confirm the impression, on the other hand, that the person can be aware of things through non-sensory means; 'faculties' of telepathy and clairvoyance are perhaps operations of the soul without dependence on the body.

'The higher level of mental life is the intellectual level as distinct from the sensory, imaginative, instinctive, or emotional', writes Father Shaw.[48] The distinction is between those functions which are subject to time and those which are not. Imagination, for instance, the faculty for creating mental images, is subject to time, since images must follow one another; you cannot make two simultaneously. At the intellectual level 'we apprehend truth and principles which are valid independently of time, and can form the concept of timeless being,' says Father Shaw.[49]

Intellectual insight, being delivered from the successiveness of time, does not belong to the animals and is that which marks spirit rather than soul. It is that which makes man congruous with God and akin to the angels. It is also at the level of spirit that we should understand the solidarity of mankind in Christ; for

> where body and soul mean plurality, separation and temporality, spirit means unity, immediacy, and simultaneity.[50]

Knowledge of the spiritual sphere is always received, never achieved; it is given from outside. It is not irrational; that is to say, spiritual knowledge received may be diagnosed and described 'in terms suitable for the non-spatial, as realistic as that which is possible on the physical plane'.[51] The spiritual is, in short, a true sphere of man's life, combining and interpenetrating with the physical and the psychic (soulish) to make up the complete person. Spiritual atrophy under the pressures of modern secularism is thus a diminishment of our humanity. In Mr Winter's terms, the 'real me' is body, soul, and spirit. When the body dies, spirit is left maimed and needs another 'body' for its full expression. What that body is was described long ago by St Paul.

What is it like to live in that body? Or is the question in itself impious, or simply impossible to answer?

Strictly, it is impossible. We cannot say what it is 'like', for we have no true likeness with which to compare it. As so often, we must say what we can say in the language of analogy. Most so-called spiritualist communications (assuming that they are genuine) illustrate the difficulty. The life they depict is little more than an exaggeration of some aspects of this present one. They are in fact not spiritual communications at all, but 'soulish' or 'psychic' ones, where the person's intellectual life is feeding on his memories. Better silence than that.

But I do not think that we can take refuge in some parable from nature and refuse to answer the question at all on the grounds that a caterpillar could not possibly know what it will be like at the butterfly stage. There is truth there, inasmuch as we cannot visualize or imagine an existence in conditions so different from our present ones. But human beings are not caterpillars; we are 'free spirits, created with a view to eternal fellowship with a personal God'.[52] The analogy is also useful in reminding us that personal identity continues; caterpillar A becomes butterfly A, and caterpillar B butterfly B. But the continuing identity of human beings 'in Christ' is that of natural beings who are already caught up into the transforming power of the Holy Spirit. Surely then we may find in our present experience of life 'in Christ' some clues which will point us reliably to certain aspects of the beyond. We should look for qualities which mark true Christian life here and now and which are capable of limitless expansion when the conditions of time and space are removed.

We do not experience a new life after death. We experience the same life of the spirit expressed in newly expanded ways.

5

We may select almost at random four out of the many sides of life in Christ, and we will consider them according to the inner logic of Evangelical Christianity. There is the joy of salvation. There is the knowledge that we are at home in the universe. There is the experience of unlimited brotherhood. And there is the transformation of powers which comes from being caught up in the Spirit.

Joy is a consequence of accepting wholeheartedly the destiny which God has provided for us. That destiny is characterized by the theological term 'grace'. We have been given through no excellence of our own a share in the new humanity in Christ. Grace is a shorthand way of recalling the total freedom of God's decisions. The choice of the human race from among all the created species of this planet to make spiritual response to him was entirely his doing; after all, other species have adapted themselves to their own environment more effectively than has *homo sapiens*. Similarly, there were many peoples in the neolithic Middle East more advanced than the Hebrews or with greater cultural promise, but he chose Abraham and his descendants. And among those descendants he could have chosen many another girl than Mary to give human life to his eternal Son. His grace falls where it chooses. It can be neither conjured up nor earned.

All that sounds rather forbidding, perhaps arbitrary and

unfeeling. Some theologians, bending words under too heavy a weight of meaning, have given that impression. They have drawn negative conclusions concerning those who were not singled out. But though Abraham's son Ishmael was rejected in favour of Isaac, he had his own different but honourable path to follow.[53] As the revelation of God's ways became clearer, it was possible to see that his exclusive choice of a minority group was made for the eventual inclusion of mankind as a whole.

Those who have received grace know that it is no burden. 'Restore to me the joy of thy salvation', sang the penitent psalmist.[54] 'My spirit doth rejoice in God my Saviour', echoed the Virgin Mary.[55] 'Graciousness by definition does not pauperize.'[56] It does not override dignity and respect for the personality; rather, by declaring the person to be worth saving, it confers dignity and establishes respect. Grace is God accepting us as we are. In accepting our acceptance, we lay ourselves open to the transforming power of His Spirit.

Joy in salvation is the condition which results from a positive response to divine grace. It is the free working of the human spirit which no longer resents God. Joy is thus more basic than outward circumstances, which is why martyrs and incurable sufferers have been among those who chiefly display it. The only rust which can eat joy is the corrosion of our acceptance when we assert ourselves against God.

Though it is a condition of the human spirit, joy is properly classified among the fruit that God's Spirit brings forth in human lives. St Paul's handling of the theme in his Letter to the Galatians[57] merits close study. Joy is second only to love and is followed by peace, patience, kindness, goodness, faithfulness, gentleness, and self-control. Those things mark those who 'belong to Christ Jesus' and among whom the power of the Spirit is working.

Exegetes point out that St Paul uses the singular when he speaks of the Spirit's fruit; the works of the flesh which he has immediately contrasted with it are plural. The Spirit unites while the flesh—Pauline shorthand for human energies insulated from the Spirit's control—divides. The Spirit's fruit thus works towards the point where the individual finds his fulfilment in relation to other people. In another Pauline phrase, it 'builds up the Body'.

The Spirit's fruit in joy begins here and now and continues like a swelling river until it empties into the sea of eternity. It is thus not incompatible with struggle, pain, or frustration. There is indeed here and now a conflict between the Spirit whose eternal powers are at work and the flesh of the old humanity in which we continue to live. Realism at that point is the antidote to any romantic disappointment over 'the saints' who are 'all too human'.

Joy as a present experience with a future climax is a mark of the Spirit's activity which Christians share with Christ. Let us, wrote the author of the Epistle to the Hebrews,

> ... run with perseverance the race that is set before us, looking to Jesus the pioneer and perfecter of our faith, who for the joy that was set before him endured the cross, despising the shame, and is seated at the right hand of the throne of God.[58]

Jesus himself, St John records, spoke to the disciples of his imminent departure in similar vein:

> Truly, truly, I say to you, you will weep and lament, but the world will rejoice; you will be sorrowful, but your sorrow will turn into joy. When a woman is in travail she has sorrow, because her hour has come; but when she is delivered of the child, she no longer remembers the anguish, for joy that a child is born into the world. So you have sorrow now, but I will see you again and your hearts will rejoice, and no one will take your joy from you.[59]

The great German scholar Adolf Harnack is said to have reduced the essence of Christianity to two great convictions: the Fatherhood of God and the brotherhood of man. The learned world has not endorsed his view, though the phrase sums up well enough what many simple people feel. Most certainly, however, both elements have an essential place in the fuller life made available through Christ.

To believe in the Fatherhood of God means to know yourself at home in the universe which is the work of his hands. It is to realize that, despite all appearances to the contrary, life is neither hostile nor indifferent nor 'absurd'.

The Fatherhood of God is thus no casual belief to be taken for granted. It is as much a mystery as any other cardinal article of faith. It has meaning at several different levels. Of the high doctrine of Fatherhood within the Blessed Trinity we will say nothing beyond a reminder that it forms the august background to all family life.[60] There is a general sense in which God is the Father of all creation, especially of the human race: a loose sense, unstressed but not unrepresented in holy Scripture.

The sense in which Jesus taught his disciples to pray to their heavenly Father is what St Paul called 'by adoption'.[61] It is essentially supernatural.

> When the time had fully come, God sent forth his Son, born of a woman, born under the law, to redeem those who were under the law, so that we might receive adoption as sons.

Our sonship to God is thus a deliberate divine appointment intimately connected with Christ and our redemption. Furthermore:

> Because you are sons, God has sent the Spirit of his Son into our hearts, crying 'Abba! Father!'[62]

To pray 'Our Father' is therefore no less than to make an affirmative response to the total activity 'for us men and for our salvation' of God, Father, Son, and Holy Spirit. Professor Christopher Evans has well commented: 'If he is Father, he is Holy Father, the Father with an almighty difference'.[63]

The notion of human brotherhood, also, is found in various forms. Stoic moralists in the ancient world and their humanist counterparts today find support for a hope of human brotherhood in the fact of a single species: not Christian man, religious man, black, brown, pinko-grey, or yellow man, but the human race as a whole. Sadly, it is far too feeble and generalized a link to serve as a basis for observing more than the simplest decencies of behaviour.

A Christian understanding of human brotherhood starts from the general fact. It finds its fulfilment in the new humanity

of Christ, for adoption into divine sonship is a virtual rebirth
into brotherhood with all the others who have received the
adoption. From there it reaches back into the general brotherhood, claiming kinship with new intensity and working for the
adoption of all human beings into the brotherhood.

The brotherhood of man provides a spur to humanitarian
concern and endeavour, but it is not primarily that. It is a
condition of human existence since the coming of Christ, who
in taking human flesh brought the entire race into a new
relationship with God. Human brotherhood is a fact whether
or not it is admitted, and indeed wherever it is denied by
man's inhumanity to man. So it is that Christians under
martyrdom have prayed with their Lord, 'Father, forgive
them, for they know not what they do.' As much as the
Fatherhood of God, the brotherhood of man is an inalienable
mark of the new humanity whose early stages powerfully affect
this present life but whose culmination lies far in the unknown
beyond.

Equally inevitable is the presence of the Holy Spirit. The
charismatic movement of our time is underlining realities of
the Spirit's presence which had lately been scarce; but he has
never been absent. Authentic Christian life cannot exist apart
from the Spirit, for 'No one can say "Jesus is Lord" except by
the Holy Spirit.'[64] The Response 'And take not thy Holy Spirit
from us' in the Prayer Book offices of Morning and Evening
Prayer, is a reminder that every act performed in the name of
Christ is a witness to the Spirit's presence.

The place of the Spirit in the new human solidarity in
Christ is most clearly seen in connection with intercessory
prayer. 'The Spirit', wrote St Paul,

> helps us in our weakness; for we do not know how to pray
> as we ought, but the Spirit himself intercedes for us with
> sighs too deep for words. And he who searches the hearts of
> men knows what is the mind of the Spirit, because the
> Spirit intercedes for the saints according to the will of God.[65]

Since intercessory prayer perplexes many contemporary
Christians, these remarks need expanding.

Intercessory prayer is not designed to inform the Deity of

matters of which he is presumed to be ignorant. Nor is it meant to deflect his mind from its inscrutable purposes. It is rather a way of expressing what being adopted into divine sonship means, and of carrying out one of the chief responsibilities which God has seen fit to delegate to his human sons and daughters. Intercession is an activity of a grown-up child, not of an infant; a grown-up child who has learned his Father's mind through being taken into his confidence. On the one hand, God has entrusted to mankind the development of much of the potential in the creation. On the other hand, the universe is not governed by laws as strictly immutable as deistic theologians or deterministic scientists suppose. Within the grand design there are many options still open. Enormous consequences for good or ill hang upon a thousand choices made each day. Here is the area where prayer can be decisive; where through the Spirit we may grasp the divine intention and pray as we ought.

The New Testament provides an example of human relationships transformed into what they will be in the fuller life beyond the present. It will be useful to consider its implications with some care, not for the satisfaction of curiosity over matters best left alone, but because the example is a window letting in light on a matter much darkened by abstraction.

The example is that of marriage and the conversation about it, reported in three of the four Gospels, between Jesus and the Sadducees. The Sadducees were that group among the religious Jews of the time who did not believe in resurrection. They tried to involve Jesus in damaging controversy—their rivals the Pharisees did accept resurrection—by asking an awkward question. Moses the lawgiver, whom all parties accepted as an authority, ordered that if a man died leaving a widow but no children to support her, any brother of his free to do so must marry her. Suppose, said the Sadducees, that there were seven brothers, the oldest of whom only was married. He died; and, through a remarkable series of deaths, each of the six eligible brothers in turn married the widow. Last of all the woman died. When the day of resurrection came, whose wife would the lady be?

Jesus's answer disclosed a principle which operates far

beyond the immediate problem. To quote him in St Luke's version:

> The sons of this age marry and are given in marriage; but those who are accounted worthy to attain to that age and to the resurrection from the dead neither marry nor are given in marriage, for they cannot die any more, because they are equal to angels and are sons of God.[66]

That reply was, of course, couched in terms and images familiar to the people of the time but requiring a measure of translation for today. But its import is plain. Jesus points out that marriage is limited in the same way that it is in the Prayer Book service. It belongs to this life. Jesus goes further than the Prayer Book in drawing a negative conclusion. Marriage does not apply beyond this life.

Marriage, we may say, is an arrangement of human relationships adapted to the needs and conditions of this present life. In particular, it contains an element of exclusiveness. The couple entering into marriage are to forsake all others, keeping themselves only for each other as long as they both shall live. A happy marriage will be one given to hospitality; but the generosity, the self-giving, will be limited. You ask a friend to your table but not to your bed. That exclusiveness is lifelong.

Many people today deny the last point. Marriage and its exclusiveness, they say, is a matter of convention, something which may be continued or revised as circumstances suggest. It is valuable, for example, when there are children, for a stable relationship between parents encourages the emotional security which children need for their personal development. But, they say, once that need is passed, the parents may without censure separate and if they so wish pair off with someone else.

Christian teaching does not disagree absolutely with the last sentiment. The disagreement is over timing. The exclusiveness of marriage lasts until death parts the couple. To suppose that marriage can end earlier is to confuse the present phase of life with the next.

The quality of difference between this life and the next, which demands an exclusiveness in marriage until death only, may be illustrated from the different ways in which things may be known. Knowledge may be by possession, or it may be by communion.[67] You may know a piece of music by possessing all manner of knowledge about it: its rhythm, its tempo, its key, its harmony, its melody, its history. You may know all that and far more without the music having any effect upon you.

A proper appreciation of the music calls for a different relationship between it and yourself: a set of attitudes which may include more or less knowledge possessed, but which will certainly involve you in being receptive, listening, being open to the music, allowing it to act upon you. Appreciating music, as distinct from possessing knowledge about it, requires that the traffic should go both ways. The appreciation of a work of art, where technical knowledge possessed is taken up to form part of an experience where the work of art 'says something' or 'does something' to you, is an example of knowledge by communion.

The distinction is one that can be made in many areas of life. In relations between people, even the briefest face-to-face meeting will include some trace of knowledge by communion. The process of 'getting to know the neighbours' is particularly interesting for the interplay between possession and communion, for it will include possessing some facts about them as well as experiences of social communion with them. They and we may well feel that there is a limit to the usefulness of such exchanges; many a pleasant social relationship has been soured by failure to see that the limit of communion has arrived.

It is in the intimate and lifelong institution called marriage that communion between two persons is carried through most fully. Knowledge by possession, of course, has its place; life, and even more literature, abounds in marriages spoiled by secrets, pockets of knowledge undisclosed to one of the partners. There is also a proper place for reserve within marriage; part of the growth of a marriage is learning to respect your partner's reticences. A healthy marriage is one where the couple's knowledge of one another, physical, social, intellectual, and spiritual, deepens by the interplay of possession and communion.

The process is one essentially between the couple concerned. However much they are the centre of an expanding family, belonging to many circles of friendship or common interest, they are at the centre on their own. Their relationship as husband and wife demands a measure of exclusiveness. It is proper for them to know each other by possession and communion to the exclusion of everyone else.

It is proper, that is, to life in this world. The exclusiveness of marriage is always in the end temporary, for death lies ahead. The exclusiveness of marriage is thus always threatened and sometimes under threat becomes aggressive. The result is possessiveness, a word with a bad ring, and jealousy. But pressures are necessary for full development even if they sometimes bring over-reaction. They are needed if only to prevent complacency.

Marriage, in fact, is always a 'becoming'. Not even the most successful has ever fully 'arrived'. There is always more to learn by knowledge, further reaches of communion to experience. Marriage is thus suited to this present life which itself is always a journey, limited by embodiment in time and space yet holding within itself unfulfilled hints of that which lies beyond.

To say that compared with life before death, life beyond it is an arrival, does not mean that the life to be is static. The eternal life which Jesus released into human life continues uninterrupted by physical death. But it is different in that it continues untrammelled by the constraints of time and space. The language of love may then be spoken without reserve. The exclusiveness which before death meant separating to each other one man and one woman no longer has meaning. There is no need for love to be in any way possessive. Indeed possessiveness is swallowed up in a communion where everyone shares to their capacity the limitless love of God. The distinction between 'sacred' and 'profane' love has vanished.

6

Joy in salvation, God's Fatherhood, and the brotherhood of man are thus permanent conditions of the new humanity being developed by the Spirit.

We are to grow up in every way into him who is the head,

into Christ, from whom the whole body, joined and knit
together by every joint with which it is supplied, when each
part is working properly, makes bodily growth and upbuilds
itself in love.[68]

They form part of the dynamic of Christian growth while the
new humanity develops into what in God's purpose it already
is. At the human level, individuals are integrated together in a
relationship which changes with the environment and which
involves 'rubbing off the corners' without destroying the
integrity of the separate person. St Paul called it 'sanctification',
the growth into holiness in response to the Spirit. It is
essentially a corporate process, the individual like a cell finding,
as it develops, its proper place in the total 'body'.

The discipline and worship of ordinary church life exists
largely to help along that process. But holiness is not an end in
itself. It is no matter of self-cultivation, whether of the individual
or of the group. From first to last the activator is God, by the
Spirit evoking response from those who are called to swell the
'body' of his incarnate Son Jesus Christ.

The process moves towards a climax. From one side that
climax looks like the fulfilment of human history, from another
it seems to come after the winding-up. From one side it is the
end of the pause, when the Son of man returns to earth from
heaven. From another it is the disclosure of the Son of man
present on earth, though hidden, in the midst of his people all
the time. Literal descriptions of this event are impossible, for it
is without precedent or parallel. The New Testament writers
press into service a large number of different myths, which
often contradict each other, but which all point to some aspect
of the truth. Later attempts to organize the New Testament
images into a coherent programme have always been disastrous.
One can only say: 'It will be like that, and that, and that, but
it is not quite any of them.'

Two major senses are present in the Greek word most often
used to designate the event, *parousia*: both a 'coming' and a
'being present'. Another word used in various forms is that
from which our 'apocalyptic' comes. There the central meaning
is 'unveiling'. The word 'eschatology', much used in recent

theological discussion, conveys essentially the notion of 'last'. The event, if you like, will be the last stage of a process. It will be the arrival on the scene of something new, which is at the same time the disclosure of that which is already here though hidden.

The parousia is the moment when Christ stands forth open and unmistakable, reigning unchallenged in majesty. Those who have opposed him will be appalled at that moment of final disclosure, when all ambiguity ceases. Those who have waited and watched and suffered will be vindicated. The moment will be one of judgement, since the true state of what has previously been concealed will appear. But, as the parable of the last judgement pointed out,[69] many will be the surprises both for joy and for woe.

The parousia will thus vindicate each human person in his or her true integrity. It will also be the vindication of man as a species. Human history from the First Adam will become intelligible as the Last Adam stands forth in his full stature and, in St Paul's great phrase, 'delivers the kingdom to God the Father'.[70]

It will be the end of a long journey. What then begins is beyond the bounds even of mythical speculation.

4

Jacob's Ladder

The Christian people is humanity in process of renewal: the pioneers, the first-fruit, the part on behalf of the whole, the sign of what one day will be. Yet the Christian people at the level of history is organized into many mutually exclusive bodies which barely recognize each other as each generation marches through its brief spell of earthly life.

But Christ's people, the new Adam that shall be revealed has a vastly wider membership in each generation than those who belong to any of the visible churches. At the end, when all secrets are open, many will be found to belong to the new Adam who had never so much as heard of it. And, sadly many who had taken their membership for granted will find that they have deceived themselves.

Christ's people, the people of God, are to be found in every generation but are confined to none. It is therefore impossible to write about the Church with any degree of theological completeness if we confine ourselves to those members of it whom we commonly call 'alive'. We will have to venture further into the interior of that mystery whose edges we earlier explored, and consider the ways in which the familiar world is bound up with the beyond.

First, a reminder about language. A Soviet cosmonaut came back from his flight into space jubilant to have found no God there. It is necessary to remind readers of this book that though they may not themselves look at the bright blue sky and comfort themselves with the thought that above it lives a friend for little children, there are many critics who think that if they are Christians, they ought to.

Heaven, we are told, is not a place but a state, the state of being where God is. Where God is, there is heaven. That definition may have its limitations, but it does remind us that the phrase 'a journey to heaven' is metaphorical. The Church is well called 'the Pilgrim people of God',[1] always on the move; but its journey is through time as well as space, and its destination is theological rather than geographical. We use spatial terms, then, with the clear understanding that they are often used metaphorically; but use them we assuredly must, or else keep silence.

A case in point is supplied by the ancient dream of Jacob's ladder.[2] Its foot was on earth and the top of it reached to heaven, and the angels of God ascended and descended on it.

> And behold, the LORD stood above it and said, 'I am the LORD, the God of Abraham your father and the God of Isaac; the land on which you lie I will give to you and to your descendants; and your descendants shall be like the dust of the earth, and you shall spread abroad to the west and to the east and to the north and to the south; and by you and your descendants shall all the families of the earth bless themselves. Behold, I am with you and will keep you wherever you go, and will bring you back to this land; for I will not leave you until I have done that of which I have spoken to you.'

Then, we read,

> Jacob awoke from his sleep and said, 'Surely the LORD is in this place; and I did not know it'. And he was afraid, and said, 'How awesome is this place! This is none other than the house of God, and this is the gate of heaven.'

I have quoted that passage at length because it highlights so many features of a proper contact between our present life and the beyond; for there are many improper ways. Before examining the episode, however, we may set beside it another, from the New Testament. Stephen has just ended his searing indictment of the Jewish authorities for betraying their trust as their forbears had so often done.

> Now when they heard these things they were enraged, and they ground their teeth against him. But he, full of the Holy Spirit, gazed into heaven and saw the glory of God, and

Jesus standing at the right hand of God; and he said, 'Behold, I see the heavens opened, and the Son of man standing at the right hand of God.'[3]

Understandably, the infuriated crowd took that for blasphemy and acted accordingly.

And as they were stoning Stephen, he prayed, 'Lord Jesus, receive my spirit.' And he knelt down and cried with a loud voice, 'Lord, do not hold this sin against them.' And when he had said this, he fell asleep.[4]

A dream and a vision, two of the classical media through which human beings have become aware of the supernatural. They occur in a wide variety of religions and cultures, and anthropologists often borrow from psychologists in order to explain them. The mechanism itself is unimportant, for the medium is not the message. If God wishes to communicate with his creatures, it is to be expected that he will use whatever medium may best convey the authority of the communication. He will speak through dreams to people who expect him to.

The context and the content are both important. Jacob had left his homeland to escape the murderous intentions of his brother Esau, and to find himself a wife of suitable stock to continue the line of Abraham. The dream came as an assurance on the highest authority that Jacob had been right to set out on his lonely path. Indeed, he was as right as had been his grandfather Abraham to leave Ur of the Chaldees. The message of reassurance which Jacob received in his dream was nothing less than a reaffirmation of the covenant which the Lord God had made with Abraham.[5]

Stephen's vision was of similar import. He was defying the Sanhedrin, who had crucified Jesus and had thus betrayed everything good that had begun with Abraham's departure from Ur.[6] 'The God of glory appeared to our father Abraham' was how he started his survey of divine choice and the disobedience of the Chosen People across the centuries. It was the same glory of God which appeared to reassure him in his hour of martyrdom.[7] His theology was hardly adequate by later and fuller New Testament standards; but he was full of the Holy

Spirit who made his vision of the Son of man standing so vivid and compelling that his last words recalled directly those of Jesus himself.

One could produce a chain of examples from the Old and the New Testament where the beyond broke in upon earthly consciousness in visions or dreams, by angels or voices. Christian history lengthens the chain to include apparitions of the Blessed Virgin, especially over the last century and a half, as well as the charismatic movement of today. They are all abnormal phenomena. The possibilities of deception are endless. We need criteria for deciding between authentic and deceptive, and perhaps between those that derive from God and those that are of satanic origin.

The matter is one of urgency far beyond the limits of church obedience. A feature of our time is a lack of confidence in historic institutions, which are widely suspected of secret interests. Venerable Christian bodies see their numbers shrink at a time when fringe religions flourish. More and more bookshop shelves bear the label 'Occult.' Interest is widespread in heightened states of mind, in mood-changing through meditation or drugs. Techniques of manipulation and control have been developed to suspend another person's rational judgement. Many of these things are in themselves neutral; their use for good or ill depends on the user. Some practices are in themselves evil. Christian theology, which claims to have first-class criteria for discerning good and evil, has a clear responsibility towards mankind.

The experiences of Jacob and Stephen show certain traits to be sought in any authentic communication from God.

First, the initiative came from beyond. Jacob did not solicit his dream, nor Stephen his vision.

Secondly, the message conveyed was no new revelation, but applied and extended one which was already part of revealed truth. It reassured the recipient in a moment of crisis that he was on the right lines.

Thirdly, it emphasized the consistency of God in his purpose, concern, and ability to see through what he had begun.

So much for the general background. In considering alleged communications through paranormal media, we should take seriously the existence of non-physical ways of perceiving. The 'psychic' sphere of human existence[8] has been neglected in recent Christian thought, and has become the province either of severely agnostic investigators or of uncritical 'fringe' religious groups. The result is that one whole side of human awareness has come to be thought of as odd, even freakish. Current interest in the occult may usefully remind theologians that

> There are more things in heaven and earth, Horatio,
> Than are dreamt of in your philosophy.[9]

We have to realize that, just as there are in the human make-up modes of awareness which do not pass through the physical senses, so there are objective entities which exist in spheres not open to investigation by the methods of sense perception. The most modern-minded of us should interrogate the old traditions as seriously as the latest teachings of psychology for enlightenment on the nature of those entities. It seems sensible also, considering the unsatisfactory state of much of the best-intentioned human activity, to hear again biblical and later teachings on 'principalities and powers' which hold mankind in thrall, on demons which cannot be driven out except by prayer and fasting.

Consider, for instance, the destructive voraciousness of a demon:

> The horror of an evil spirit is its emptiness and its activity of expressing it. Into that emptiness it gathers all that is deformed, degraded, and can feed its pride and lust to express itself. . . . Cast into the earth, its intelligence will try to realize itself in that which is congruous to itself, and to build up in time and space through the instrumentality of human energy a kingdom for itself in opposition to the divine light, and so a kingdom of darkness.[10]

The idle curiosity which empties a mind to see what happens may open the door to the most unpleasant squatters. Warnings against dabbling in the occult cannot be too strong: you do not have to believe in demons to be possessed by one.

We should, however, beware of panic. There are certain

parallels between our own time and the period in European history from 1450 to 1700. Both are periods of particularly intense discovery of how the natural order works. Both are times of religious upheaval and social change. Both are conscious of occult influences corrupting human life.

One difference between that period and our own is that the Christian Church, though inwardly divided, was politically strong in whatever form was locally dominant; and it countered the occult powers with the savage repression of the witch-hunt. The historian Norman Cohn has recently published a fascinating 'psycho-dynamic' study of the origins of that grim phenomenon, *Europe's Inner Demons*.[11] He traces one powerful background factor in a chapter entitled 'Changing Views of the Devil' Of the demon-obsessed teaching in the later Middle Ages he remarks: 'It is a far cry from the confidence of the early Christians.'[12]

The early Christians also were greatly troubled by the attacks of demons, but they were convinced that Christ was manifested that he might destroy the works of the devil.[13] The Middle Ages were more realistic than the moderns in expecting to find pockets of demonic hostility. Their failure lay in not claiming the victory which Christ had already won. Not the least valuable service which the charismatic movement is doing the Church today is to discover the confidence of the early Christians against the unseen foe.

'Both angels and demons', insists Fr Gilbert Shaw, 'are to be distinguished from disembodied human spirits.' He calls attention to the absence of anything new in alleged spiritualist communications.

> What is presented in this way is not a world of angels reflecting the glory of God, but a screen of deformation between God and the man made up of human error and the delusive arguments and solicitations of demons ... Not the immediacy of spirit but a vault of separation, to shut out the truth of God in and through the imaginings of human speculation.[14]

Father Shaw is perfectly clear that the barrier, whether demonic or the work of deluded and malignant human spirits, has been broken finally and for ever by 'the coming into space-time of God himself in the flesh-taking of the Son.' He asserts, therefore, that the original Christian test of spiritual health proposed in the New Testament is still valid in the twentieth century. The heightened interest in the occult in the twenty years since Father Shaw wrote has meant the repetition in some form of most of those ancient views of Christ which minimized his victory over the evil powers. The truth of any view about God and man needs to be established by St John's test:

> By this you know the Spirit of God: every spirit which confesses that Jesus Christ has come in the flesh is of God, and every spirit which does not confess Jesus is not of God.[15]

Or, as St Paul says:

> Now concerning spiritual gifts, brethren, I do not want you to be uninformed.... Therefore I want you to understand that no one speaking by the Spirit of God ever says 'Jesus be cursed!' and no one can say 'Jesus is Lord' except by the Holy Spirit.[16]

Or, in words attributed to the Lord himself:

> Jesus ... asked his disciples ..., 'Who do you say that I am?' Simon Peter replied, 'You are the Christ, the Son of the living God.' And Jesus answered him, 'Blessed are you, Simon Bar-Jona! For flesh and blood has not revealed this to you, but my Father who is in heaven.'[17]

In this, as in all ages, the acid test of all Christian pretensions to spirituality is simple: does it acknowledge the full materialism of the incarnation, the flesh-taking of the Son of God which diminished neither his divinity nor his humanity?

2

The ladder which Jacob saw in his dream stretched from earth to heaven. The angels were ascending and descending it, and at the top stood the Lord repeating the former promise to his people.

The scene may remind us of mankind's true place in the scheme of things, set in the midst with part of him in the spiritual realm, part in the material, between God and the beasts. It also serves to remind us that we are not the only spiritual creatures in existence, for before us, our elder brothers in the created order, are the angels who have no material part. It is also a reminder that although human beings are firmly set within the structures of time and space, there is about us that which transcends time and space, finding total fulfilment only in the beatific vision of God, the pure and eternal Spirit.

The divine promise communicated in Jacob's dream, that his descendants were to be the means whereby all mankind found blessing, points forward to the totality of God's action for our salvation: being born into our race in the Person of his Son; breaking the power of all that holds the species in bondage through the victory of his life-giving death; raising his Son to intercede for us at the right hand of power; sending the Holy Spirit to form Christ among his People until the day of vindication.

The dream reminds us also that human destiny is not simply an individual matter. Jacob was an individual with his own problems; but he was also one of 'the fathers', an early link in the chain which led to the Second Adam, into whom the human race was to be incorporated for salvation. The individual human being is of infinite importance, but he will only realize his full promise in the company of his fellows. 'Man's chief and highest end is to glorify God, and fully to enjoy Him for ever',[18] but the beatific vision may be seen only in company.

Meanwhile we are on the march, the Pilgrim people of God in its wanderings. We must not be suborned or tempted out of the way by lurking pockets of evil. We must test the spirits whether they be of God: do they confess that Jesus Christ has come in the flesh, or do they shy at the downright assumption of flesh by spirit?

'In this connection', writes Father Shaw, 'we should remember what the early Church saw so clearly, that the fullest safeguard of the truth is a sufficiency of devotion to our Blessed Lady, the giver of the flesh, as Mother of God, Queen of angels and the glory of the saints. For she is the second Eve and her foot is on the serpent's head.'[19]

Finely said, though hardly surprising; for Father Shaw was an Anglo-Catholic priest of the stricter sort. Splendidly orthodox, his catholicism owed more to the 'western tradition' than to the Book of Common Prayer or the Thirty-nine Articles. He was writing well before the Second Vatican Council, and few members of the Church of England outside his own circle would have shared his sentiments.

Yet he was right. Now that Rome has bent so well-tuned an ear to Protestant difficulties, she has put forward a number of authoritative texts which make it possible for Catholics and Evangelicals to discuss the matter of our Lord's mother in a calm and brotherly spirit. For when the Council decided by a narrow majority to scrap an independent *schema* on our Lady and to include its teaching in the constitution *On the Church*, the runaway doctrine (as it had seemed to the outside Christian world) took its important place in the team. No longer was Mariology to be a branch of theology with its own rules and its own logic, but a doctrine whose significance was once more defined in relation to Christology, to the Holy Spirit, and to the Church. It was related, much as were other doctrines, to the Scriptures, and so could be discussed as part of the total system of belief.

Inter-confessional discussion has not indeed proceeded as far or as fast as might have been hoped. Despite the encouraging progress of the Ecumenical Society of the Blessed Virgin Mary,[20] the Protestant world in general still thinks of Mariology as an alien growth. Mary herself is recognized as a vital character in the gospel story, but for Protestants her importance lies wholly in the past; she is not to be reckoned a force in present-day discipleship. Certainly she is not someone to whom one should have 'a sufficiency of devotion', whether or not as 'Mother of God, Queen of angels and the glory of the saints.'

I have stated elsewhere[21] my reasons for breaking completely with a negative Protestant attitude, and indeed for claiming at least some statements of the distinctively Catholic doctrines and some forms of Catholic devotion for the enriching of Evangelical religion. In terms of contemporary theological debate, Catholics and Evangelicals are natural allies against 'radical' interpretations of the faith which aim to eliminate its supernatural elements. The things which Catholics say about Mary as mother of God safeguard the things which Evangelicals say about her Son.[22]

But 'Queen of angels' and 'glory of the saints'? Father Shaw's choice of epithets neatly indicates those aspects of our Lady which bear on the subject of this chapter. 'It is foolish to speculate on what happened to Mary's body', declared Ambrose Autpert, an eighth-century abbot, in the course of a sermon on the assumption,

> seeing that no one doubts that she is raised above the angels and reigns with Christ. It should suffice that she is truly called Queen of Heaven, because she has given birth to the King of Angels.[23]

Angels, as we have seen, are essentially and always servants of God. However exalted, they have no independent purpose. In the course of their duties, we may say, they played their part in the divine plan of redemption through the incarnation of the eternal Word. So the archangel Gabriel visited Mary at the annunciation. But Mary, having accepted her supreme role of co-operating in that redemption, is raised (to speak in the foolish human manner) to take precedence over the entire angelic order. Reflection upon that circumstance will deliver us from that confusion between angels and the spirits of the faithful departed which has done so much by its sentimentality to discredit the supernatural elements in the faith.

So far as I am aware, 'glory of the saints', unlike 'Queen of angels', does not occur in any of the traditional litanies of our Lady, but it is none the less relevant. I have elsewhere expounded the 'theological life' of Mary in terms of St Paul's great affirmation of God's consistency.

> For those whom he foreknew he also predestined to be conformed to the image of his Son, in order that he might be the first-born among many brethren. And those whom he predestined he also called; and those whom he called he also justified; and those whom he justified he also glorified.[24]

Surely Mary's conception might be seen as the beginning of that series and her assumption as its culmination. Mary would then be the woman whose predestination has, in view of her unique role in giving the Son of God his flesh, been advanced to its full term of conformation in the image of that Son; Mary who was called and who replied, 'Let it be to me according to your word'; Mary who was justified and rejoiced in God her Saviour; Mary who has been brought to the point of glorification. 'If it may be so taken', I concluded,

> 'and Mary may be seen as the one of us who has already "got there", then it gives great force to the insistence of the Vatican constitution [*De Ecclesia*] that Mary is a sure sign of hope and solace for the wandering People of God; and it makes her a splendid trophy of the gospel's grace and power.'[25]

Yet, it may be replied, that is all very well. It is no doubt possible to interpret Mariology in those terms. But is it not very sophisticated, an intellectual's approach? Marian devotion, on the other hand, is above all the fervent religion of simple people. Is it not a cult which flourishes in local forms, attached to particular statues, Our Lady of This or That? Wells and groves are indeed involved, places which have been taken for holy from pagan days. Has the face which hides behind the tinsel and votive offerings any real connection with Mary of Nazareth; or does it belong to some ancient goddess appearing now in crudely Christian dress?

It is encouraging to find similar doubts expressed and answered by no less an authority than Pope Paul VI. His apostolic exhortation *Marialis Cultus* deals with Marian doctrine and devotion as it was found some ten years after the Vatican Council.[26] He notes that some Catholics have almost ousted the holy Virgin from their scheme of things while others have promoted exaggerated devotion. He endorses warmly the Council's decision to state its doctrine about Mary in the context of the Church understood as the Pilgrim People of God; and he indicates that theologians could usefully concern themselves with her particular connections with the Holy Spirit.

A papal exhortation is a pastoral letter addressed to all bishops in communion with the see of Rome. It is thus particularly striking to find so strong an ecumenical emphasis:

> ... the ecumenical aspect of Marian devotion is shown in the Catholic Church's desire that, without in any way detracting from the unique character of this devotion, every care should be taken to avoid any exaggeration which could mislead other Christian brethren about the true doctrine of the Catholic Church.[27]

And again:

> ... We are glad to see that in fact a better understanding of Mary's place in the mystery of Christ and of the Church on the part also of our separated brethren is smoothing the path to union.[28]

Even more encouraging to a Protestant Christian is the Pope's concern over the trivial and thoughtless nature of some traditional Marian practices, and his determination that sentimental and other unworthy elements in popular devotion should not reduce the purity of the Church's doctrinal standards.

The triviality has social and psychological roots. Mary, the submissive woman, can reflect too easily male chauvinist hopes. It is refreshing to find that His Holiness grasps so firmly the nettle which he calls 'the discrepancy existing between some aspects of this devotion and modern anthropological discoveries and the profound changes which have occurred in the psycho-sociological field in which modern man lives and works.'[29] 'In the home', the exhortation continues, 'women's equality and co-responsibility are being justly recognized by laws and the evolution of customs.' The adverb 'justly' is especially welcome.

The decline in Mary's popularity, which concerns the Pope, is in this document attributed to her traditional image as a pious *Hausfrau*. The bishops are bidden to examine the problem. The Pope himself contributes three useful observations. Mary is not commended for her particular life-style, let alone for her socio-cultural background; but rather, for her responsible acceptance of God's will, an act and an attitude which have 'a permanent and universal exemplary value'.[30] Secondly, the most familiar, and the most readily objectionable, pious representations of Mary 'are not connected with the Gospel image [of her] nor with the doctrinal data which have been made explicit through a slow and conscientious process of drawing from revelation.'[31]

The Pope then sketches an impression of Mary which sets her essential characteristics as found in Scripture beside the woman of today: sharer in decision-making, responsibly choosing continence, proclaiming God's vindication of the humble and oppressed. 'The modern woman', we read, 'will recognize in Mary ... a woman of strength, who experienced poverty and suffering, flight and exile ... These are the situations that cannot escape the attention of those who wish to support, with the gospel spirit, the liberating energies of man and society.'[32]

It would, however, be wrong to conclude that the familiar picture of Mary as a mother concerned first and last with her Son is to be replaced by one of her as the secular champion of Women's Lib. The result is rather the disclosure of Mary as the 'woman whose action helped to strengthen the apostolic community's faith in Christ', an allusion in particular to the part which she is reported to have played in the wedding breakfast at Cana, 'and whose maternal role was extended and became universal on Calvary.'[33] The scene is thus set for a theological and devotional concern with Mary which will engage directly with the human condition of today.

Evangelicals will be particularly interested in the Pope's handling of popular Marian religion. Popular religion becomes a problem increasingly as its anchorage in theology grows weaker. How best to cope with it is a perennial preoccupation of pastoral care, a problem as much for Protestants as for Catholics. Popular religion becomes an actual danger when its eccentricities are made the jumping-off ground for new theological statement. Protestants should walk warily here lest they fall into the snare of self-righteousness. It is easy to pick on some bizarre local custom in Marian devotion. Such things are colourful and exuberant, and are therefore easier to spot than are the lower-key, moralistic quirks of sober Protestant Christianity.

'Time makes ancient good uncouth', observed the American sage.[34] 'The Church understands that certain outward religious expressions, while perfectly valid in themselves, may be less suitable to men and women of different ages and cultures' is how *Marialis Cultus* puts the same point.[35] The document is not a theological treatise but a pastoral letter; very properly it deals gently with unsophisticated religious sensibilities. But 'certain attitudes of piety which are incorrect' are made aware that the velvet glove conceals something harder:

> The Second Vatican Council has already authoritatively denounced both the exaggeration of content and form which even falsifies doctrine, and likewise the small-mindedness which obscures the figure and mission of Mary.[36]

It is a pity that the translation, unusually good over most of the document, begins to labour at this point; for the matter is of outstanding importance ecumenically.

> The Council has also denounced certain devotional deviations, such as vain credulity, which substitutes reliance on merely external practices for serious commitment. Another deviation is sterile and ephemeral sentimentality, so alien to the spirit of the gospel that demands persevering and practical action. We reaffirm the Council's reprobation of such attitudes and practices ...[37]

The Pope's argument, it will be noticed, has moved beyond a simple admission that time has made ancient good uncouth. He is no longer updating practices to make them socially and aesthetically acceptable. His concern is with truth both in doctrine and in living, truth which he sees in certain quarters being compromised by falsehood. False attitudes and practices must be identified and expelled; for

> they are not in harmony with the Catholic faith and so have no place in Catholic worship.[38]

His Holiness spells out the reasons for insisting on 'careful defence against these errors and deviations'. The discrimination required will give to Marian devotion a solid base in theological doctrine, and consequently will lessen the attractions of 'the exaggerated search for novelties or extraordinary phenomena'. It will rescue the historical and objective figure of Mary from the ravages of legend, which must be eliminated. It will help the development of a devotion which will match doctrine; hence the need to avoid one-sided presentations. And finally

> it will make this devotion clear in its motivation; hence every unworthy self-interest is to be carefully banned from the area of what is sacred.[39]

The devotion of the credulous is all too easily manipulated in one interest or another.

Evangelicals who were startled by Gilbert Shaw's reminder of how a right regard for Mary could safeguard the right view of Christ which is the touchstone for 'testing the spirits', may therefore be reassured. Whatever may have been the case earlier, whatever dark pockets may still remain, the highest authority in Rome has determined that the Catholic faith shall not mutate into Mariolatry. She is firmly linked with her Son who is her saviour.

The base in revealed theology being thus secured, we may pass to another matter which has with good reason worried Evangelical Protestants: the fear that to enter into some sort of Christian relationship with our Lord's mother or with other saints in glory betrays a lack of trust in Christ as the only Saviour. To buttress the Our Father with the Hail Mary ('Holy Mary, mother of God, pray for us sinners, now and at the hour of our death') seems an infinitely tragic version of the man who wore a belt in case his braces should break.[40]

Let it be said at once that any notion that our Lady is easier to 'get round' than her Son is instantly to be dismissed. Her will was completely identified with his, and so indeed must be those of all the saints in glory; for the glory is his, and they would hardly share it if they did not also share his will. There is only one road to the Father and that is the Son.

Recourse to the prayers of the saints in glory is not fundamentally different from asking the prayers of our Christian friends on earth. We ask especially the prayers of those whom we believe to share most closely in the mind of Christ; and if that is the case within the circle of our Christian friends on earth, how much more eagerly should we welcome the prayers of those who are with Christ in glory. The true intent of such prayers is well conveyed in the responsory which ends the Angelus and other Marian devotions: 'Pray for us, O holy Mother of God, that we may be made worthy of the promises of Christ.' We do not turn to Mary and to the other saints by way of an alternative to Christ; the effect of such prayer is to quicken, clarify, and renew our trust in him.

3

We approached the figure of Mary after Fr Gilbert Shaw's suggestion that a right regard for her as mother of God was a safeguard in 'testing the spirits' according to the New Testament standards; for by no means all that claims to be 'spiritual' comes to us from God. I have pursued the matter further, because so many issues of importance meet at some point the person of our Lady. Certainly that is so in the matter of relationships between all those who are 'in Christ' in this life and beyond. In some of the ancient litanies Mary is addressed as 'Neck of the Body'. The term may raise a smile, but it has something to say. For Christ is the head of his Body, the Church; and she, as the member of the Church who has (by her unique connection with him, and the way she was prepared for it) 'got there first', may be the means by which we see into the darkness which lies beyond this life.

And light is sorely needed. Evangelical religion has little to say beyond the assurance that in Christ there is life and salvation and joy where without him there is death and destruction and despair. In that, of course, Evangelical religion is entirely correct. But it is so blinded by the glory of Calvary that it fails to make room for one consequence of God's love: God grants to the people whom he has saved the dignity of working out in themselves their own salvation.[41] Evangelical religion supposes that Catholic teaching on purgatory detracts from the completeness of Christ's finished work on the cross by leaving over something for the sinner to add.[42] But purgatory is not a middle state somewhere between hell and heaven. It lies, if you like, within the bounds of Greater Heaven. It is the state where the saved become in God's mercy what they ought to be so that they may enjoy without hurt the beatific vision.

It is a pity that Evangelicals understand Catholic teaching so much in terms of the Reformation controversies, for they deprive themselves thereby of the strength which they should derive from true fellowship with the departed. Their negative approach prevents them from playing a full part in the total fellowship of prayer. In certain cases it can cause grave unhappiness and even drive them to the false and forbidden comforts of spiritualistic practices.

The teaching of the Second Vatican Council is far more true to the biblical witness.

> When the Lord comes in His majesty, and all the angels with Him (cf. Matt. 25.31), death will be destroyed and all things will be subject to Him (cf. 1 Cor. 15.26–7). Meanwhile some of His disciples are exiles on earth. Some have finished with this life and are being purified. Others are in glory, beholding 'clearly God Himself triune and one, as He is.'[43]

The seventh chapter of *De Ecclesia* is short out of all proportion to its importance. For here we find the conception of the Church as God's People, called according to the new covenant and established in Christ, described theologically in terms of this life and beyond, both of them related according to the total sweep of God's total purpose. 'The Eschatological Nature of the Pilgrim Church and her Union with the Heavenly Church' is the chapter's title, 'eschatological' having the sense of 'pertaining to the last times' when history will draw to a close and God's final Kingdom will be inaugurated.[44]

Looked at in the perspective of individual destiny, the new humanity appears divided into three groups: the pilgrims on earth, the sufferers in purgatory, and the triumphant in heaven. The separation of those groups from each other is in fact tempered by their unity. For

> in various ways and degrees we all partake in the same

love for God and neighbour, and all sing the same hymn of glory to our God. For all who belong to Christ, having His Spirit, form one Church and cleave together in Him (cf. Eph. 4.16). Therefore the union of the wayfarers with the brethren who have gone to sleep in the peace of Christ is not in the least interrupted. On the contrary, according to the perennial faith of the Church, it is strengthened through the exchanging of spiritual goods.[45]

There seems to be no reason why that 'exchange' should be interrupted by physical death, as Protestants so often assert. On the contrary:

By reason of the fact that those in heaven are more closely united with Christ, they establish the whole Church more firmly in holiness, lend nobility to the worship which the Church offers on earth to God, and in many ways contribute to its greater upbuilding ... Thus by their brotherly interest our weakness is very greatly strengthened.[46]

From early days the Church on earth has prayed for her dead. The help which by our prayers we can give to those who are being purified seems slight compared with the help that we (and no doubt they) receive from those who have already joined our Lady in the actual perfection of Christ. But the mutuality is important. It is a two-way traffic of care and concern, a genuine 'exchange of spiritual goods:' as it were the life-blood of love circulating round the entire Body of Christ. In the words of a footnote to the Vatican text, 'Prayers for the dead and the veneration of the saints take on an added meaning when viewed not simply individualistically but, as here, in an ecclesial context.'[47]

The Council was, of course, aware of Protestant fears lest attention paid to the saints might somehow detract from that paid to Christ. But this is to forget that the saints are saints only because they have been so transformed by Christ and their wills identify with his.

By its very nature every genuine testimony of love which we show to those in heaven tends toward and terminates in Christ, who is 'the crown of all the saints'. Through Him it tends toward and terminates in God, who is wonderful in His saints and is magnified in them.[48]

'Let the faithful be taught, therefore,' said the Fathers, anticipating another Protestant objection,

> that the authentic cult of the saints consists not so much in the multiplying of external acts, but rather in the intensity of our active love. By such love, for our greater good and that of the Church, we seek from the saints 'example in their way of life, fellowship in their communion, and aid by their intercession'.

The last phrase, which sums up the traditional understanding of the 'spiritual goods' which the Church on earth derives from the saints, is quoted from a liturgical preface. The Council goes on to insist that communion with the saints enriches rather than weakens, let alone proves a substitute for, 'the supreme worship we give to God the Father, through Christ, in the Spirit'.[49]

Before turning to consider that worship, one question must be asked. Why, if it be true that the Church has always looked to those who have died close to Christ for their prayers, is there no record of the fact in the New Testament? Those who oppose the practice, of course, answer that it is not mentioned because it was an early corruption and so had no place in authentic Christianity. The tone of my argument so far no doubt suggests that I disagree.

The explanation lies, I believe, in that delay in the return of Christ which was contrary to very early Christian expectations.[50] It was only with the passage of time that the number of Christians who had died began to exceed the living. Part of the adjustments needed in Christian thinking caused by the need of the Church to continue indefinitely as a body within history concerned the relationship between the living 'in Christ' and the departed. There were no controversies about it in the early Church. The practice of venerating the heroes of the faith seems to have unfolded without crisis as the Spirit led the Christians into the further implications of their fundamental faith.

The question which later controversies have raised for ecumenical theology is, of course, that of the extent to which the canon of Scripture stands over against and in judgement upon the Church's tradition, and how far it should be read within that tradition; a matter which we will take up later.

4

We have indicated sufficiently the good company in which the Christian is included for time and beyond it, and in which the Church militant, so often beleaguered, knows itself to be part of something enormous. We have, however, said little about the Church as the representative new humanity, the Adam re-created in Christ.

There is little that we can say with certainty beyond the fact that it is so. The Church is no less than the Body of Christ and that is the new humanity. The manner in which those ultimates connect with the Church in its identifiable boundaries is an aspect of the mystery which has not yet been revealed. Certain principles may be postulated. The first is that no definition of the Church smaller than that of the new humanity is finally tolerable. The second is that there is no salvation for mankind outside Christ, so that all who form part of the new humanity must in some way be vitally related to him. Various terms have been coined recently to explain how this may be so, notably 'the latent Church' and 'anonymous Christians'. Such terms infuriate the serious unbeliever, and they must not be used in such a way as to imply the overriding of human choice.

Two brief points may make the paradox easier to live with. Belief is not simply a matter of intellectual assent, and truth is a matter of deeds as well as of words. It is possible for someone's 'general direction' to be set towards Christ while the intellect is conditioned invincibly throughout this life against him. It is not unfair to see the surprise of those in the parable of the last judgement who found themselves unexpectedly among the sheep, as a moment of 'deconditioning'. Secondly, the new humanity is a given state. It exists through the will of God and does not depend upon our awareness of it. It is something which the individual human leaves, if at all, only by deliberately contracting out. The evangelistic and catechetical function of the Church is to make him aware of what he is and to live accordingly.

It is time to return to Jacob's ladder and to consider again the angels who were ascending and descending upon it. Christian tradition knows of two ways in which angels regularly cross our path: in the special attachment of guardian angels, and in their worship of God, in which human worship has a share.

Perhaps there is no point where Christian teaching has been so trivialized as in the matter of guardian angels. They are particularly associated with children and have suffered from the Victorian and later cult of sentimentalizing childhood. Unfortunately the more recent trend of a more matter-of-fact approach towards children, seeing them as persons to be respected in their own integrity, has been developed by people undisposed to take angels seriously. It is a pity, in view of Jesus's defence of childhood. St Matthew's version includes the phrase:

> See that you do not despise one of these little ones; for I tell you that in heaven their angels always behold the face of my Father who is in heaven.[51]

The value of a guardian angel is his access to God ('behold the face of my Father . . .'), which enables him to intercede on behalf of his charge as well as generally protect him.

Some of the early Christian Fathers believed that only children had guardian angels. The protection was withdrawn from the grown person, perhaps so that he could prove himself unaided in the Christian struggle, being eligible thereby for greater glory.[52] Two passages from the scanty New Testament teaching suggest the contrary. The first was the reaction of his friends to the sudden appearance of St Peter whom they supposed to be in jail. 'They said, "It is his angel!" '[53] This shows at least the popular belief at that time. The other is an indirect argument which emerges from recent study of the Gospels. The verse about the little ones and their angels (Matt. 18.10) does not occur in the corresponding passages of

Mark and Luke. Furthermore, in Matthew it is separated from the denunciation of those who cause children to sin by verses 7–9, which deal with temptation and the means of resisting it. The Revised Standard Version reflects recent opinion when it makes v. 10 start the paragraph, which includes the parable of the man who leaves ninety-nine safe sheep to go after one that has gone astray. That parable ends: 'So it is not the will of my Father who is in heaven that one of these little ones should perish.' In that instance 'little ones' would more naturally refer to disciples generally, (cf. 'little flock'[54]), regardless of age or youth.

The guardian angel's function of praying for his charge is an easy extension of the general angelic function of prayer and worship. The earliest Christian view is reflected in the Apocalypse of St John:

> Then I saw the seven angels who stand before God, and seven trumpets were given to them. And another angel came and stood at the altar with a golden censer; and he was given much incense to mingle with the prayers of all the saints upon the golden altar before the throne; and the smoke of the incense rose with the prayers of the saints from the hand of the angel before God.[55]

Christian worship is thus a new note, the song of the redeemed, taken up into the chorus of praise and adoration which goes back to the first angelic creation. Again, St John's vision shows the connection:

> Then I looked, and I heard around the throne ... the voice of many angels, numbering myriads of myriads and thousands of thousands, saying with a loud voice, 'Worthy is the Lamb who was slain, to receive power and wealth and wisdom and might and honour the glory and blessing!' And I heard every creature in heaven and on earth and under the earth and in the sea, and all therein, saying, 'To him who sits upon the throne and to the Lamb be blessing and honour and glory and might for ever and ever!' And the four living creatures said, 'Amen!' And the elders fell down and worshipped.[56]

The song of the Lamb is a 'new song' (v. 9) taken up into the song of the whole creation. It was sung by angels and other figures in the court of heaven, who were then joined by

> a great multitude which no man could number, from every nation, from all tribes and peoples and tongues, standing before the throne and before the Lamb, clothed in white robes, with palm branches in their hands, and crying out with a loud voice, 'Salvation belongs to our God who sits upon the throne, and to the Lamb!' And all the angels stood round the throne ... and they fell on their faces before the throne and worshipped God, saying, 'Amen! Blessing and glory and wisdom and thanksgiving and honour and power and might be to our God for ever and ever! Amen.'[57]

What John saw in his vision is institutionalized in the Church's liturgy:[58] 'Therefore with angels and archangels and with all the company of heaven we laud and magnify thy holy Name.' The reformed worship of the Prayer Book never lost sight of the truth that Christian worship here on earth is caught up into the worship of the entire creation. It has to be admitted, though, that the depredations of Reformers anxious to stamp out idolatry, and of the Puritans a century later, made of the English parish church a hard place in which to realize that truth. The paintings and statues of a Catholic church, the icons which are essential to the Orthodox liturgy, make it far easier for today's worshipper to know himself part of a vast activity to which he makes his small contribution.

This is perhaps the point of furthest penetration into the secret of Jacob's ladder. 'Surely the Lord is in this place', the patriarch said with fear when he awoke. 'This is none other than the house of God, and this is the gate of heaven.' The ladder up and down which the angels travelled joined together heaven and earth, showing that both of them were the Lord's house. We are back in that world at which we looked earlier, the Jahwist's view of human origins. Perhaps he was not so naive when he pictured the Lord God walking in the garden in the cool of the day. After all, it was the Lord's own garden.

We cannot begin to answer adequately modern man's difficulties over worship: the activism which sees no value in silent contemplation, the hearty extroversion which 'sends up' heaven as an eternity of hymn-singing tedium, the scepticism concerning institutions, the dismissal of the old and tried. We offer merely a pointer or two, indicating where ancient ways may speak to today's concerns. They concern the nature of glory.

Worship is essentially a matter of giving glory. And glory is essentially the substance of something, its true worth, its true weight. To give glory to someone is therefore to ascribe to him his true worth. Giving glory to God is thus not a matter of flattery, however much it might be so in the case of a human potentate. It is a matter of insight and honesty. To give glory to God is to confess him for what he is. For us, that means Creator, Redeemer, Lifegiver: the maker of all the vastness of that which is accessible to sensible knowledge, and of that which is not accessible to it. It means acknowledging him to be the universal Creator who knows when a sparrow dies, when a hair falls from our head; the universal Creator who has adopted us to become his children. The theme is not easily exhausted.

Another pointer is that the whole creation gives glory to its maker. The rhythm of being, when that which is created functions in accordance with the laws of its own nature, is a form of worship. Mankind for all its greatness arrived late on the created scene. The proportion of worship articulated in human terms is thus minute. The song of creation is mostly wordless; part of the human destiny is to give it words. That theme too is not readily exhausted.

There can be no adequate worship which is confined to a single human generation. Novices such as the generation living on earth at any given moment can but lisp the nursery rhymes. True worship needs the experience of every generation to give it the body and the variety proper to its theme; and even the total human contribution must be taken up into the angelic song to give it the spirit and the truth needed to present it to the eternal Spirit. Our praises may well be true, but they are necessarily so small that they barely fill the earthly liturgies, let alone those of heaven. So in God's mercy the great ones who constantly behold the Father's face take our praises and turn them in a way that unaided we never could.

5

Militant Here in Earth

It was impossible to write the last chapter without a feeling of dismay. In God's good purpose all Christian people, all mankind indeed, have been formed into a goodly company stretching from here to eternity. It is a company in which man's God-like potential for creativity and joy and love may be developed to the full. Yet here on earth the members of that company are divided among themselves, shut into their self-sufficient denominations, sometimes cold and indifferent to each other. Their history has been appalling. The church militant seems to spend much of its energy in civil war.

The last section of this book must therefore be addressed to matters of Christian unity.

I hope that I shall thereby remove one of the commoner causes of frustration which afflict those who read theological books: that of having been taken through a long and complex argument only to be left dangling. Those who have followed my path thus far through matters concerned largely with the beyond and the hereafter are entitled to ask, 'So what?' If my comments cause exasperation of another kind, they have at least an immediate and practical Christian reference.

There will no doubt be some who consider that in arguing for devotion to the mother of God and the saints, I have gone back on the Reformation. How, they may ask, can he urge those things from a position which he calls Evangelical? The question is entirely proper and I have often asked it myself. In what follows I shall therefore draw more than I have previously done on personal considerations, though I believe that my reasons are capable of more generalized expression.[1]

It is misleading to suppose too complete a difference between Catholic and Protestant. The differences are no doubt greater than two tips of an iceberg, but they are certainly based on an enormous fund of common belief. All the great Reformers accepted, for example, the doctrines of the Trinity and the incarnation in their traditional form, which all the principal denominations include in their confessions of faith. It was different with many left-wing religious teachers and communities in the sixteenth century, just as it is with many para-Christian groups today.[2]

John Jewel, Bishop of Salisbury, was perhaps the most typical theologian of the Elizabethan Settlement. His *Apology of the Church of England*,[3] a copy of which was ordered to be placed in every parish church, repeatedly claims that the Church of England was teaching the true Catholic religion and that the papists were the innovators; the Fathers, he believed, were on the Reformers' side. Luther's spiritual experience which touched off the German Reformation came from a study of the New Testament according to principles which he had learned in his monastic studies. Calvin's dogmatic system owes a great deal to St Augustine.

The religious dynamic of Protestantism was in fact a return to elements in the Christian tradition which had been overlaid in the recent past. It is widely recognized now that the early sixteenth century was a time when many Catholics saw the widespread need for reform.[4] Despite obstructions, political and national, it would have been possible, perhaps as late as the Council of Regensburg in 1543,[5] for the Catholic Church to have so reformed itself that, theologically at least, there would have been no need for continued separation. But when the Council of Trent met, it was too late. A new generation of reformist Catholics who had never known the zeal of earlier days had grown up with the Lutheran schism as an accepted and threatening fact. Instead of a Catholic Reformation throughout the Church, the Counter-Reformation so organized its formulations as to exclude the Protestants. The lines were fast, and both sides developed without friendly contact.

In spite of appearances, it was not to be expected that the lines would remain hard for ever. Protestant and Catholic have now lived apart for centuries, have developed their own ways often so as to exclude the other. Yet both have been responding as Christian bodies to changes in the world which included both of them, and there are unexpected resemblances; eighteenth-century Methodism, for instance, had its counterpart in the warmth (and sentimentality) of devotion to the sacred heart. And almost at all times there have been some in each camp who were prepared to respect the Christian integrity of the other.

Evangelicals within the Church of England have commonly found it hard to approach Catholicism except as a system to be opposed. Definitions are notoriously difficult, but for the purpose of this discussion we may say that Evangelical religion centred mainly upon knowing Jesus Christ as personal Lord and Saviour. Unfortunately such phrases lend themselves to cheapening by repetition. But, however it be expressed, authentic Evangelicalism will embody in some form the two elements expressed classically by the phrases 'receiving Christ' and 'walking with Christ'. Those terms relate to a personal, individual experience, but they have an inescapable social corollary: relationship with Christ involves relationship with everyone else in a similar position.

Evangelicals within the Church of England look back over the centuries since the Reformation in one of two ways. They may begin from a very clear impression of New Testament Christianity, finding in the writings and their Old Testament background a potential dogmatic system which was most faithfully articulated by the Reformers, especially perhaps John Calvin. There is a royal line of scriptural orthodoxy connecting the two. What lay between them was less good, for the true knowledge of God and salvation was often partially masked or even eroded. Even Augustine of Hippo, the greatest name between St Paul and Calvin, was at certain points sadly emmeshed in the theological decadence of his time.

Such Evangelicals are above all theologians. They are Christians formed by the Word of God and they have the greatest respect for words. Accuracy of statement, purity of doctrinal line are the safeguards of orthodoxy, which is rendering God the glory due to him through holding the right opinions about him. They are therefore impatient with a holy intolerance of any compromise which may blur the clear light and lines of what God has caused to be revealed. That revelation was admirably stated in the great Protestant confessions.

Other Evangelicals are less sure that true obedience to God is always tied to intellectual formulations about him. They are more concerned with the inwardness of religious experience, and are happy to recognize the same experience whatever the theological structure in which it is housed. Intellectually, they are less sure that they have understood New Testament Christianity correctly; or that the Reformers had; or in what sense it is normative for subsequent Christianity. They believe that in the sixteenth century the Western Church was so corrupt that many hungry souls were not fed, and that those who discovered the true Bread of Life were sometimes driven out of the organized church.

The first group, whom I shall call 'absolute Protestants', see an integral connection between Evangelical religion and Protestant theology. I shall call the second group 'relative Protestants', for they believe that the Reformation positions preserved Evangelical religion at a time of extreme danger, but that Evangelical religion may well exist in its integrity within other theological frameworks. Obviously, I belong to the second group.

It is possible for a relative Protestant to say that the Reformation has done its work. Indeed one would expect that the need for it would one day be ended. The existence of Protestant Churches independent of the mother Church of the West should be a temporary phenomenon.

Does that mean 'going back on the Reformation' in the sense that the dividing of Christendom then was a mistake? Yes, in that the dividing happened because people at that time prized other things above the Church's visible unity; in retrospect, a curious and rather unattractive mixture of theological conviction and political advantage. It is, however, unprofitable to try to apportion blame, for with hindsight we are able to see things more clearly than would have been possible at the time. More constructively, we may say that if that for the sake of which Protestants were prepared to break the unity of the Church has been put right, then on that ground at least the division should end. It has done its work.

Is it right, then, for Evangelical Protestants to seek reception in the Roman Catholic Church? That would be one solution. But it depends on several factors. Even if it is now possible for the Evangelical essentials of the Christian life to be fostered unhindered within the Roman obedience, the passing of time has raised other questions which would need affirmative answers. Neither Rome nor the Protestant Churches have stood still since the sixteenth century. Rome has defined its teaching office to the point where the successor of St Peter has been declared beyond all ambiguity, if within narrow limits, infallible. Two major doctrines about Mary, in the middle Ages generally received as pious opinions, have been declared to belong to the inner core of belief which is essential to salvation. The Evangelical needs to be persuaded not only that those beliefs are true, but that they have been properly proclaimed to be part of the essential core; and also that the authority which thus proclaimed them was itself properly proclaimed to belong to that core. He will need, in short, to return an affirmative answer to three questions. Has Rome purged herself of those errors which caused the divisions of the sixteenth century? If so, have the claims which she makes for herself come to look inherently likely? And if so, are they fulfilled in the Roman obedience as it is now developing?

The Protestant Churches also have developed. They have taken on responsibilities and acquired traditions. To speak of the Church of England only, the Church of the Elizabethan Settlement is still the national Church. It has responsibilities towards far more citizens of this country than its actively supporting members. A distinctive religious culture has grown up, embodying values in architecture, music, and literature as well as in a style of Christian living which is very distinctive. The gradual attrition of the Church of England by individual conversion to Rome would diminish the rich variety of Christian obedience.

It is in any case most unlikely. Individual conversion will be the answer for those for whom it has become an overwhelming personal imperative. If they are persons whose judgement deserves respect, then to back their belief that the Reformers' objections to Rome have been met by their own change of allegiance may well advance the cause of unity. But unity will not come from the total of mass individual conversions. It must be a corporate relationship between the organized bodies concerned.

The call to Christian unity has never been more compelling than at present. In an age of technological culture spiritual concerns must earn their right to be heard. Christianity claims to have a gospel of reconciliation and renewal, an offer from God for all mankind. If its representatives are not reconciled among themselves and resist renewal by clinging to ancient divisive issues without challenging them, the credibility of their message must suffer; their way of life shouts so loud that the world cannot hear their words.

If the Church of England deems it right to survive as an independent body and is serious in its wish to bring the Gospel to today's world, it must have something distinctive and worthwhile to offer, something whose preservation is more important than ending division between the Churches. Given its particular history, it must first decide whether there is still need to bear witness to reformed Catholicism, or whether the Roman Catholic renewal of recent years has rendered that need obsolete.

2

The present book would not have been written but for the changes which have come over the Roman Catholic Church during the last fifteen years. It is true that an Evangelical could always find Catholic writings which illuminated the common faith. It was possible to meet an individual or even a group of people who shared the same concerns. But the institution remained hostile, and the congenial people seemed always to be going against its grain.

The first element in the change is Rome's new willingness to listen to criticism. As a young Anglican of Evangelical sympathies who could speak French, I found myself in the 1950s welcomed at conferences, especially in France and Belgium, where Roman theologians would talk with a frankness that surprised me. They were anxious to hear my reactions to matters such as infallibility, the place of bishops, the ministry of the laity. There was no attempt to persuade me of their views. Their wish was rather to discover those points where I could not follow them, and to see if there was any way of rephrasing their doctrine to make it acceptable.

Reflecting upon these experiences, I realized that I was being introduced to a technique that was well advanced, for in addition to Anglicans senior to me (few of whom, unfortunately, were other than Catholic-minded in their sympathies) there were French Reformed, German, Swedish, and Church of Scotland theologians who had long been engaged in such 'dialogue'. The Orthodox, Russian and Greek, were of course involved; indeed the Benedictine Abbey of Chevetogne, where regular studies took place, was especially dedicated to fostering links between Orthodox and Catholic spirituality. The underlying method was simple: to state one's own case with the intention of hearing (impossible to convey the exact shade of meaning in *se mettre à l'écoute*) the reaction invoked in other Christians.

When Pope John called the Second Vatican Council, many of the 'experts' who advised the bishops were veterans of such ecumenical dialogue. The Pope himself was determined that the Council should be overheard by separated brethren, a phrase which took on a new meaning. The presence of observers from other Churches and the place in St Peter's which they were allowed to occupy undoubtedly made sure that those positions which were likely to give unnecessary offence to Protestant susceptibilities were suitably re-phrased.

We must not romanticize the Council. It was a Council of the Roman Catholic Church, 'ecumenical' in that domestic sense only. It did not discover 'ecumenism' in the wider sense. Long before the Council began, many of the bishops as well as their advisers had been alert to the problems of the modern world, and were well aware of the community of concern which they shared with Protestants. The Council's documents, moreover, were hammered out between Catholics of all persuasions, among them the very conservative. Those documents were often conservative in substance even when their language avoided conservative and polemical phrases.

Nor are those documents which have proved seminal on the Church, on Ecumenism, on Revelation 'radical' in the sense which that overworked word has come to bear in post-conciliar Catholicism. On the contrary, the value of those documents lies in the fact that they represent the solid, essential positions of historic Catholic teaching, free alike from concessions to secular modernity and to anti-Protestant polemic. They are exciting because they show to how great an extent solid, 'straight' Catholicism says what an Evangelical wants to say. I mentioned earlier how surprising it is to have one's worries over Marian exaggeration formulated by the Pope himself.[6] It will be remembered how closely in the previous chapter I was able to base an exposition of the communion of saints upon the appropriate chapter of the Vatican constitution *De Ecclesia*.

Rome has, in short, shown how to be loyal to the received tradition even while listening with all seriousness to the outsider's constructive criticism. A phrase from Pope John's opening address to the Council is of the utmost importance for appreciating the ways in which Roman Catholicism since then is new, and the ways in which it is not new:

> The substance of the ancient deposit of the doctrine of faith is one thing. The way in which it is presented is another.[7]

It is quite wrong to suppose that Rome has changed her views on any matter concerning the substance of faith. But a great deal depends on its presentation, not merely on the language used, but also on the context in which a doctrine is expressed. (The implications of Mariology, for instance, are different since the subject has been set firmly within the doctrine of the Church.) The tone has quite changed. If Protestant formulations in turn could be rephrased to avoid anti-Catholic content, it could well be that the two approaches to such doctrines as those of grace and justification would be found to be complementary.

A second feature of recent Roman Catholicism is its pluralist character. Right up to the eve of Vatican II the Roman Catholic Church had seemed monolithic, a huge, timeless structure turning one and the same face to every human situation. That monolithic quality was indeed the reason why some Western intellectuals, weary of the uncertainties and changing moods of Protestantism, turned to Rome. The ancient Latin tongue symbolized her universality. The decision to break with Latin had a traumatic effect on many such people, though it is remarkable how easily most Catholics, especially 'cradle-Catholics', have entered into the spirit of the change.

No longer is Rome monolithic. At almost all levels of theological sophistication comes an understanding that truth is many-sided, that the single formulary can hardly express the whole.

Scholars have looked again at the early history of the Christian Church to see in detail how the varying schools of teaching handled the differences between them: which differences broke the unity between the centres which taught them, and which were allowed in a spirit of 'agreeing to differ'. The early Church made its mistakes, but a historical view which sees the result as well as the course of ancient controversies is able to learn from the mistakes as well as the successes. Bishop (later Cardinal) Willebrands, in a paper read to the Anglican–Roman Catholic joint Preparatory Commission in 1967, cited Charles Moeller's conclusions over one such dispute:

> The Byzantine sixth century is of decisive importance for the history of the schisms which were to arise later. It teaches us a lesson valid for our time as well as for ancient times: that various theological schools must co-exist peacefully within the single tradition of the Faith. The unity of the Church is not to be confused with outward uniformity, no more than with the triumph of one theological school.[8]

Mgr Moeller's study was published as long ago as 1954. His conclusion is in line with Pope John's distinction between the substance of a doctrine and the way that doctrine is expressed. The Council's documents contain a number of phrases which suggest that Christian doctrine is a complex structure which includes more and less important parts: a 'hierarchy of truths', in fact.[9] The notion of 'pluralism' of expression within a basic unity of the faith allows a great deal of space for ecumenical manoeuvre, for theologians are not tied to a single agreed formula. When Catholic theologians remember that there exists 'an order, or "hierarchy", of truths, since they vary in their relationship to the foundation of the Christian faith', the way is indeed open for 'a kind of fraternal rivalry to incite all to a deeper realization and a clearer expression of the unfathomable riches of Christ (cf. Eph. 3.8).'[10]

The discovery of Rome's own pluralism, important as it is for inter-Christian relationships, is even more significant for the energy which it is releasing in her own life. For the Roman Catholic Church is herself as wide as the world. All nations, all cultures and all social classes are represented in her. It is only to be expected that Catholics from different backgrounds will express their obedience in different ways. In the past there has been some pressure to conform to a Western European model. If the central authorities can do justice to the belief that differences of expression can be a proper response of fundamental obedience, the Catholic Church will be well on the way to removing the deepest-seated objection to the credibility of her claims, namely, that in practice her unity is fundamentally juridical and legal.

The Vatican Council, of course, found the source of Catholic unity in a very different place:

> By her relationship with Christ, the Church is a kind of sacrament or sign of intimate union with God, and of the unity of all mankind. She is also an instrument for the achievement of such union and unity.[11]

Brave words, and ultimately true. But they must be seen in the Church's life to be true as well as proclaimed to be so. The giving of due weight to her own inner pluralism is a stage on that way.

For Protestants, the most crucial theological change is that concerning revelation: how God has made known his truth; and the corollary, how we may be sure that, amid all the conflicting versions of the truth, what we have received is authentic.

The received picture is of a total wall separating Catholic and Protestant. Against the Reformation assertion 'From Scripture only' the Council of Trent declared 'From Scripture and the tradition of the Church'. In the nineteenth century tradition was firmly located in the papacy. 'Tradition? I *am* tradition!' said Pius IX, the Pope under whom both Mary's immaculate conception and papal infallibility were made dogmas binding the faithful upon pain of damnation. Against all of which Protestants continued to open the Bible. Every Protestant theologian was brought up on that deadlock.

It is not always realized how far the deadlock has been loosened by changes within Protestantism. There are, no doubt, some who still wield the Bible as a uniform oracular weapon. But they are a minority, at least in the great Churches of the West. Most Protestants now accept that the Bible is a human book, however much it may convey the Word of God. Further, it is not a book, but a collection of very disparate books approaching a common theme from a hundred different angles. It is possible to go to the Bible and pick out of it very different messages. It all depends on what characteristics you decide are so important that they must be the dominant ones round which you organize the others into coherence.

In the early centuries the possibilities were reduced by the decision that those passages which implied that Jesus was from the start the eternal Son of God should take precedence over those which implied that he was a man whom God took up into his special service. It was further decided that the God who figures in the Old Testament was the same as the Father of whom Jesus spoke. It followed that God throughout the Bible must be understood as Three and One, Father, Son, and Spirit; that Jesus was the Word made flesh, the Second Person of the Trinity who came into human life in order to redeem it; that after his ascension the Holy Spirit came upon the Church and empowered it for its journey through history, preaching the gospel to all nations and to every generation.

That was not the only possible interpretation, but it was the one which in the first four hundred years of Christian history defeated its rivals. It was the one according to which the Reformers read their bibles. For they began their journey to the independent stands they would adopt, not with independent minds, but informed by the Catholic life and teaching in which they had been educated. There were, indeed, other and more radical reformers who refused to accept the correctness of that interpretation, but they were opposed, and indeed persecuted, as much by the great Reformers as by the Catholics. They are not our concern in the present discussion.

The Reformation, then, accepted the Catholic tradition in all basic or fundamental theological matters. The phrase *scriptura sola*, 'by Scripture alone', meant 'by Scripture interpreted according to the great tradition'. The Reformers insisted that they accepted it not because of the tradition, but because the scriptures themselves on internal evidence demanded to be taken that way. Modern Protestants are not so certain.

The concept of 'the Scriptures' has itself been brought into question. Why those books and no others? It is easy enough to answer that question for the Old Testament. By the time of Jesus, the Jews had become very much the people of the Book, divided into the Law, the Prophets, and, perhaps less clearly defined, the Writings. Thus the canon or yardstick was already formed, and the first Christians as good Jews simply took it over.

The New Testament was formed gradually, over the first two or three Christian centuries; though by A.D. 200 all but a few books were 'in'. The choice had been, the Reformers believed, a process of divine selection whereby the Holy Spirit guided the early Christians to complete the canon of Scripture with some of the writings which their life had called forth. Where the Catholics said that the scriptures were selected by the emerging authority of tradition, the Protestants believed that the scriptures were the God-given means of checking tradition for deviations and unauthorized additions.

By 1950, when, on the authority of tradition, Pope Pius XII proclaimed the dogma of the assumption, Catholics and Protestants alike were finding difficulty with their time-honoured positions. The pace of biblical study had quickened since the same Pope had in 1943 allowed Catholic scholars to take a full part with their Protestant colleagues. Tradition, it had been found, was itself a concept within Scripture and, what is more, one that had played a big part not merely in the selection but in the formation of Scripture. The sense in which the scriptures were 'regulative' was therefore due for review. By the eve of the Vatican Council, both Protestant and Catholic biblical scholars were at work in constructive dialogue on such problems.[12] The lines which had hardened at the Reformation were fluid again. It would be too much to claim that by 1978 agreement had been reached; but few thoughtful Christians today are prepared to assert that their position is exclusively right, and few will refuse to hear suggestions from the other side of the Reformation line.

The Vatican Council itself made one major contribution. The dogmatic constitution *De Revelatione* is a modern classic. The text makes it quite clear that there is one source of revelation, not two: God, who alone can reveal his handiwork in the natural order and his particular plans for the world's salvation, has done so in a series of personal dealings with human beings. Tradition and Scripture are both ways in which this revelation is conveyed.

> Sacred Scripture and sacred tradition form one sacred deposit of the word of God, which is committed to the Church.[13]

The Church is equipped with a *magisterium*, or living teaching office. This organ

> is not above the word of God, but serves it, teaching only what has been handed on, listening to it devoutly, guarding it scrupulously, and explaining it fully by divine commission and with the help of the Holy Spirit; it draws from this one deposit of faith everything which it presents for belief as divinely revealed.[14]

Protestants will wish to scrutinize that carefully; the notion of a *magisterium* is not immediately congenial. They should, however, look for its equivalent in their own system. It is unlikely that they will not have one. They will reflect also that when the *magisterium* is defined, it is open to scrutiny as an unofficial register of approved opinions may not be.

> It is clear, therefore, that sacred tradition, sacred Scripture, and the teaching authority of the Church, in accordance with God's most wise design, are so linked and joined

97

together that one cannot stand without the others, and that all together and each in its own way under the action of the one Holy Spirit contribute effectively to the salvation of souls.[15]

The constitution takes a high view of inspiration in its account of how and why the scriptures came to be written, but without disregarding the personal characteristics of the human authors. So high is the view, indeed, that inspiration is said to include inerrancy. The text cites 2 Timothy 3.16, but in the Greek form; the inerrancy is 'for the sake of our salvation', not absolute. The descriptions which follow of Old and New Testaments might have been written by a moderately conservative Protestant scholar; and the final section on 'Sacred Scripture in the Life of the Church' might be read with profit by any Christian.

Dr Frederick C. Grant contributed a Protestant 'response' to the constitution in the edition made under the general editorship of Walter M. Abbott, s.j. He mentions several places where he would have liked the recommendations to be more specific, but he writes from a background of warm appreciation.[16] All Protestants will wish success to the Council's wide encouragement of Bible-reading throughout the Church.

Perhaps the least that may be said ecumenically of this document is that it provides material which theologians of separated bodies might use for renewing their own confessional positions.

It will be well at this point to recall a distinction by no means new in Catholic theology, that between faith, or doctrine, and devotion. John Henry Newman made use of it a century ago in his celebrated exchange with Dr Pusey:

> By 'faith' I mean the Creed and assent to the Creed; by 'devotion' I mean such religious honours as belong to the objects of our faith, and the payment of those honours.[17]

It is possible to believe without feeling devotion, he added, but not to be devout without faith.

The distinction is not one commonly made in Protestant teaching. Its adoption would prevent some of the commoner misunderstandings of Catholic practice, and would also help Protestants to understand better the differences among themselves.

The concept of devotion is far more specific in Catholic than in Protestant religion. The devout Protestant will find himself gripped by some aspect of the truth as he has received it in Jesus. He will very often find the starting point in some phrase of Scripture. His mind will play upon it until it becomes a part of himself; he 'feeds on the Word of God', he walks by its rule, he lives in its confidence. Quite simple people often find themselves captivated by a particular doctrine which speaks directly to their particular condition, so that a phrase such as 'By grace you have been saved through faith; and this is not your own doing, it is the gift of God'[18] becomes a direct experience. Protestants will refer to such a process as 'the devotional reading of the Bible'; they will consider it altogether different from Catholic devotions.

That difference, however, is less than might be supposed. It is in part psychological; Protestants tend to meditate on concepts, Catholics through images. Newman again is helpful:

> I do not claim for the generality of Catholics any greater powers of reflection upon the objects of their faith, than Protestants commonly have; but, putting the run of Catholics aside, there is a sufficient number of religious men among them who, instead of expending their devotional energies (as so many serious Protestants do) on abstract doctrines, such as justification by faith only, or the sufficiency of Holy Scripture, employ themselves in the contemplation of Scripture facts, and bring out before their minds in tangible form the doctrines involved in them....[19]

Catholic meditation tends thus to be more pictorial, more concrete, than Protestant. Its results are easily formalized into traditions of teaching built around a particular devotional focus. It is a natural development for adherents of a particular devotional tradition to be joined in an institution; and that in turn readily builds up its own history, its own emphases. The teaching of St John Eudes, for instance, is an extrapolation from devotion to the sacred humanity of our Lord, and communities of men and women have been formed around it. But 'the sacred heart of Jesus' is in no sense an addition to the doctrine of the two natures of Christ. To quote from the introduction to the English edition of the teaching which lies at the root of this devotion:

> For St John Eudes, as for all Catholics, the ultimate object of all devotion is God, in the unity of His divine nature and in the Trinity of His Persons. But God sent His Only-begotten Son to redeem and save mankind from the penalty of sin. Through Jesus Christ our Lord and Saviour and through Him alone can we mortals have access to divinity. All the life of Christians, therefore, is centred in the Word of God made flesh. Yet it extends to all Three Persons of the Blessed Trinity and, by participation, to all persons, places and things made holy unto God.[20]

Devotion is secondary to faith. It is a means of entry whereby frail mortals are able to take a place in the vastness of divine truth. Devotions ebb and flow, they may come and go. They may be regarded as expendable, useful only while they lead into the truth. One man's meat is another man's poison, and there is nothing desirable in devotional uniformity as such. Temperamental and cultural factors have their place in devotional expression; it is here, and not in the area of faith or doctrine, that 'relevance' is important. The area of tolerance is wide; a Christian may decline to follow some devotional way without either judging those who follow it or in turn incurring their censure. Potentially, indeed, the situation is, in the devil Screwtape's phrase, 'a positive hotbed of charity and humility'.[21]

The same principles may be applied to assess the several distinctive Protestant and Evangelical devotions; for example the emphasis on the blood of Jesus in the East African and other revivals, the several teachings on holiness, and patterns of response to the Holy Spirit's activity. Sadly, intensity of Evangelical devotion has commonly led to schism upon schism, for the devotees have assumed that theirs is the only valid response to the grace which they have received.

Misunderstanding arises when devotion is confused with

doctrine. Protestants may be forgiven if, upon a quick glance at the exuberant variety of Catholic devotion, they are thus misled. If they will take a longer look, they will find that a real danger exists that devotions will distort fundamental doctrines. Catholic teachers are equally aware of the danger, and during and since the Second Vatican Council control of doctrine over devotion has been vigorously reasserted. Problems nevertheless remain. The French lay theologian Jean Guitton deals with them most sensitively.

The first problem is that caused by the 'popular' nature of many devotions, especially in parts of the world where Christianity is something of a 'folk religion':

> If our civilization were to founder, and learned infidels were to rummage in the earth where our churches lay sleeping, bringing to light statues of the Virgin and the saints, they would conclude, very falsely, that this cult of the saints was almost the whole of our religion.[22]

Guitton admits the perplexity of the modern mind confronted by such 'lower forms of religious awareness'. Yet he insists that, while what the Protestant would roundly call 'superstition' is a genuine danger, devotions even of the cruder kind have a function to perform, that of bringing down the transcendent truths of faith into the earthiness of our everyday lives. Mere knowledge, he points out, is rarely a stimulus to love.

> If we would receive a truth into our very being, into the very texture of body and soul, into that which is, as it were, the *flesh* of the spirit, the best way is to use some natural bias, to discover for it an affinity. Some sort of echo, to what is most deeply embedded in our nature.[23]

Guitton draws on Bergson's concept of a 'mediating image' to develop the type of cognition which underlies the need for devotions in the life of faith: an image 'almost material in that it can already be seen, almost spiritual in that it cannot be touched; a phantom that haunts us as we explore some new theory, a phantom from which we must seek the decisive sign, the mode of approach, the significant point to watch'.[24] 'A formula such as this,' says Guitton, 'may help to explain the function of devotion in religious experience; for devotion is just such a personal and communicable image, providing a viewpoint of the total truth of faith and thereby rendering it more easy to assimilate. Such imagery, common to learned and ignorant alike, is often the only means by which simple souls can grasp the faith in a way that is capable of influencing their lives.'[25]

The second remaining problem is aesthetic; not only the bad taste and shoddiness of the *bondieuserie* which forms the furniture of much Catholic devotion, but also the more subtle aesthetic difficulty caused by the public display of what is essentially personal and private. Devotional writings are the writings of love, devotional practices its gestures. They belong within the family circle. The expression of love, moreover, varies between one family and another, one period of time and another; that which in its own context speaks the deepest sincerity may ring hollow and false elsewhere. Newman put the problem unforgettably:

> Burning thoughts and words are as open to criticism as they are beyond it. What is abstractedly extravagant, may in particular persons be becoming and beautiful, and only fall under blame when it is found in others who imitate them. When it is formalized into meditations or exercises, it is as repulsive as love-letters in a police report.[26]

Love expressed crudely is surely preferable to precision that stays cold.

3

If Anglicanism still has a reason for surviving as an independent force in the Christian world, it must have something to offer which is worthwhile and distinctive. Historically, that 'something' has been a form of Catholic Christianity reformed according to the priorities of Scripture and the early Church, adapted to responsibilities within the English nation, and extended to other responsibilities which developed elsewhere. If the spirit of Anglicanism is to survive within its structures, the 'something' which it offers will be an organic development from what it has hitherto been.

The changes in the Church of Rome bear closely on the matter of the Anglican future. For classical Anglicanism was largely defined over against Rome, considered as a Church to be at least sick, at worst apostate. Her health is now well on the road to recovery, if not fully restored. What should the Anglican attitude be now?

It might seem that the arguments which I have earlier advanced lend support to the Anglo-Catholic movement. I suggested that Evangelical religion is weak for lack of firm understanding and belief concerning the relationship of living and departed 'in Christ'. Anglo-Catholics have said that for years. Is it not a question, therefore, of reviewing the substance of the faith as it is taught, noting those elements which have been maimed or distorted by ancient Protestant polemic, and generally 'rounding up' the faith and practice of the Church to an acceptable level of Catholicism?

At that point I find difficulties. Anglo–Catholism in its development since about 1850 does not seem to me an organic extension of the Church of England from Jewel to Hooker, Laud, and Keble. It has played down the calling to be the Catholic Church of the nation, which was its essential genius, and aspired instead to be a 'branch' of an arbitrarily defined 'Catholic Church'. The result is the growth of an episcopal sect. A second, related, difficulty is that Anglo–Catholicism is, as Cardinal Newman rightly saw, but a stage on the way. Its true fulfilment lies in the reintegration of the national Church with the Roman communion. If that indeed be the aim, then the movement has been of great value. But if an indefinitely prolonged independent Anglican presence is the aim, then Anglo–Catholicism is a confusing diversion. Any truly valuable contribution to the Christian mission will come from its Protestant inheritance.

That part of me, therefore, which is devoted to the Church of England that I know, registers dismay over some of the recent ecumenical triumphs. 'Agreed statements' between Anglicans and Roman Catholics on such thorny matters as the Eucharist and the ministry make me wonder what we are standing for. The Series III Communion Service has abandoned most if not all of those elements in the Prayer Book service which the Reformers valued above their own lives. The widespread desire for intercommunion with the Roman Catholic Church implies that all is well; if it is, surely we should go home there with all convenient speed. But has the English Reformation so fully done its work?

One group, currently vigorous in the Church of England, who clearly think not are those whom I earlier called absolute Protestants. They will probably not accept the positions which I have advanced, considering that the errors of Rome are as detestable as ever. Grateful though they will be for the occasional shaft of light in dark places, they 'could not contemplate any form of reunion with Rome as she is'.[27] The position remains fundamentally unchanged from that of the sixteenth century. They will feel, for instance, that the present Pope's insistence upon transubstantiation in his encyclical *Mysterium Fidei* shows that on one major matter at least Rome has still to tread the path of repentance.[28] They will believe that the Church of England has abundant reason for holding to the reformed Catholicism of Prayer Book and Articles, and will resist as falsehood any attempt to minimize the differences with Rome. At the same time, they will not be isolationist; they rejoice at signs of biblical reformation in Rome and welcome the possibilities of dialogue on the basis of Scripture.[29]

Others believe that, though the ground has shifted from that of the sixteenth century, there are still matters which need to be opened up in the spirit of the Reformation. The relative positions of clergy and laity within the total body of the Church militant is one such matter, and one of increasing urgency.

The sixteenth century was a time when society was organized on a strictly hierarchical basis. In England, Queen Elizabeth was faced with daunting problems of social control in a country which had no bureaucracy, poor communications, and a long tradition of turbulence. Among the clergy she found a group of people who could be controlled and whose recognized place in the community would form a stable element in every parish. Reformed theology might have much to say about the priesthood of all believers, insisting that ordination was to a ministry of the word, not to a sacrificing priesthood; but the clergy were to be a distinct order within secular society, complete with their own discipline, privileges, and responsibilities. They had their place, and once they were ordained to it, there they stayed. The remarkable continuity of the English clergy through all the vicissitudes of the sixteenth and seventeenth centuries owes arguably more to assumptions about society than about theology.

That society has now vanished, taking with it its assumptions. The question can no longer be avoided: what is a clergyman/ priest/ minister, and how is he related to other members of the Church? An answer which is both Protestant and episcopal has yet to be heard.

It has in fact been masked for over a century. The movement which led to Anglo–Catholicism was a response to the first rumblings of the final collapse of Queen Elizabeth's Settlement in Church and State. The 'age of enlightenment' combined with the industrial revolution to question the Church's privileged position in society. The movement began by emphasizing the Church's legal rights; but instead of going on to see how both rights and responsibilities might be adjusted to meet the needs of changing society, its main interests shifted in the direction already mentioned.[30] The professional status of the clergy was understood in more specifically sacramental terms, which enabled it to survive yet another turbulent century.

Today, when inflation's icy blast has freshened the already cold winds of secularism, the question can no longer be avoided. As long ago as 1960 Bishop John Robinson called for the investigation of three lines which he found dividing clergy from laity.[31] Since then the 'professional line' has been well and truly breached with the widespread ordination of men who continue to earn their living in secular occupations. That very fact has, however, thrown into greater prominence the Bishop's second line of division: the legal standing of the clergy. What is the difference between a cleric and the man (or woman) authorized to minister as a reader? Ordination. And what is the difference between the reader and the deacon?

The latter's ordination makes him legally a clergyman, but he is not allowed to perform any ministerial function which the reader does not do. The Bishop's third barrier was what he called 'the most closely guarded line of all, the sex line'.[32] At the time of writing the ordination of women is a burning issue throughout the Anglican communion.

Another matter which should be raised is that of the duration of ministry. For reasons which, as we have seen, are sociological as well as theological, it is assumed that ordination is for life. The Catholic tradition understands that ordination confers a 'character' additional to and as permanent as that conferred by baptism. The ordained man is therefore irreversibly set apart from his unordained fellow Christians. That teaching did not commend itself to many of the Reformers. The insistence of the Anglican Articles that holy orders are not to be classed with baptism throws the onus of proof on those who believe that an indelible character is imparted in Anglican ordination. That assumption is indeed widely made today. Clear-sighted Protestants will wish to distinguish the sociological from the theological elements in that assumption.[33]

The matter is not simply theoretical. The fact of late vocations to the ministry is widely recognized, and as a result many men render excellent service to the Church for the second half of their working lives. Conversely, why should not a minister undertake pastoral work for ten or twenty years followed by a change in a secular field of service? Ordination, after all, is not a matter of taking a vow. Many clergymen do find it right to leave the ministry. Others discover ways of 'opting out' without formal severance. Probably many more are prevented from doing so by lack of qualifications for other work. In most cases where there is no hint of scandal the change is accompanied by a cloud: a sense of unhappiness, failure, even betrayal.

A continuing Protestantism would question the assumption that a call to ministry is for life. It would be prepared to investigate episcopal ordination to short-term ministries. In so doing it might discover patterns of Christian obedience which could not be pioneered under present Catholic principles, but which might later be built in to an expanded Catholic order to the benefit of the whole Christian people.

It would also, of course, be bold in its investigation of women's rightful ministry within the Church.

4

Protestant action of the kind I have suggested would probably disrupt the Church of England as it now exists. In so doing, it would remove the Church's claim to be at once Catholic and Protestant and to be in consequence a means of drawing together Christian bodies who stand beside it on each flank. I am less moved by that argument than I would have been a few years ago.

It had been reasonable to suppose that the national Church was the rallying-point for Christian unity in this country. Anglican theology had followed a consistent development since the years between the two World Wars. It was generally felt that within the Church there were two broad streams of opinion, the Catholic and the Evangelical. Each of them ranged from conservatively held positions to ones which allowed great flexibility. In the middle, there was much exchange. In addition, there were those who held such extremely 'liberal' opinions that many spoke of a third group, the modernists. But between them all a consensus was possible.

The Second World War brought home as never before how pagan the population of Britain had become. The difference between Christian and non-Christian was far more serious than that which divided Christians, who must hasten therefore to resolve their differences. There were also issues which badly needed a common Anglican decision, notably that of inter-communion with the Church of South India, which recently united episcopal and non-episcopal elements, including several Anglican dioceses.

The Archbishop of Canterbury, Dr Fisher, made history with a sermon preached at Cambridge in 1946. He asked whether Free Churchmen could not, as a basis for unity, 'take episcopacy into their system'. He further set up teams of theologians to answer the question of what episcopacy meant, and to sort out other matters which continued to trouble divided

Christendom. The result was three reports which make fascinating reading: *Catholicity*,[34] representing the Anglo-Catholic interest; *The Catholicity of Protestantism*,[35] a Free Church outlook; and *The Fullness of Christ*, which expressed a fairly liberal Anglican Evangelical point of view.[36] The present Archbishop of Canterbury, Dr Coggan, was among the signatories of this last; his predecessor, Dr Ramsey, had signed *Catholicity*.

The 1950s and '60s saw several attempts to unite the main British Churches. Teams of theologians appointed by their denominational authorities met over long periods of time. The Anglican–Presbyterian talks were mainly between the national Churches of England and Scotland, involving also the smaller Presbyterian Church of England and Scottish Episcopal Church. They produced a distinguished report, but it came to nothing. The Anglican–Methodist conversations also proved abortive. The Church of England's failure to accept the scheme may well have marked the death of consensus theology.

The Anglican–Methodist proposals were defeated by a coalition of conservative Catholic and Evangelical interests. Argument centred on the morality of being ambiguous. Anglicans were unable to agree among themselves whether Methodist ministers were adequately ordained. A form was therefore devised for the mutual recognition of ministries, which was so worded that those who believed that they were in effect laymen could interpret it as ordination, while those who believed that they were already ordained could take it as an extension of ministerial commission. Supporters of the device believed that in a situation where apparently only God knew for sure what was needed, he could be asked to do it without precise instructions. Opponents considered it to be disingenuous and, other matters of uncertainty being also involved, carried the day.

Events had overtaken the scheme. The real issues confronting the Christian world of 1968 were very different from those of ten years earlier. The older distinction between Catholic and Evangelical had paled beside the rift opening between radicals and traditionalists. The radicals were thought to be so convinced of the need to update the Church and its faith that it was a question of 'beginning all over again'.[37] The Anglican–Methodist proposals were held by many traditionalists to smack of the radical impatience with theological doctrine and suffered accordingly. Their traditionalist supporters were left in an embarrassing position.

The type of ecumenical endeavour where representatives of two bodies come together to form a unity on a national basis, which will in turn serve as a nucleus for a larger unity, has fallen into the background. The creation of the United Reformed Church from the English Presbyterians and Congregationalists has been one of the few successes; significantly, the United Reformed Church has already in its turn taken steps towards wider unity.

Two apparently contradictory trends have replaced the national schemes for unity. On the one hand, unity is sought on the very local level, the several denominations in a neighbourhood doing as much as they possibly can together. The other trend is a marked strengthening of denominational ties across the world, and the Anglican Communion is among these denominations. A feature throughout the world has been the failure of schemes for national union, which have often foundered upon questions of property and its ownership. It seems that the national level no longer forms an acceptable 'middle term' between the local neighbourhood and the multi-national denomination.

I think it is a pity. The failure to consider religious allegiance nationally argues a failure in responsibility to the nation. The Anglican Communion is a late and accidental growth, bound up with the imperial phase in English history. I see no reason why it should demand a greater or more lasting commitment than the British Commonwealth of Nations, and I welcome the signs that Anglican leaders in, for instance, Africa are increasingly identifying their concerns with those of their own country rather than with those of their fellow Anglicans. I believe that the idea of unity behind the Church of South India (or, slightly later, that of North India with its firmer insistence on episcopacy) was right. The Christians of a particular country belong in one ecclesiastical

body together. If there is a conflict between such local
loyalties and lateral ones, the local ones are paramount.

The special genius of Anglican Christianity is, I believe,
national, not denominational. Throughout the Middle Ages
Ecclesia Anglicana had been a singularly independent part
of the Western Church, closely identified in its own development with that of the English people. The English Reformation
was a response to the circumstances of the sixteenth century, at
once theological and political; for in its own way the sixteenth
century, like the best Christian thought today, refused to draw
lines between sacred and secular. It was God's world, and its
earthly rulers ruled by divine permission.

The concept of the Christian nation has been too often
caricatured and dismissed as if the caricature had represented it
adequately. The 'state connection' has been dubbed 'Erastian'
as if, once that word had been pronounced, there remained
nothing to be said. The result has been the Church's
clamour for independence of the state and a desire to limit
its services to those who respond to its message: in a word, to be
a sect among other sects. The wish to see the Church an
efficient and self-contained body functioning on its own terms
as a voluntary society within a secular state is reasonable and
not ignoble. In many lands it is the only possible arrangement. But in England it is a betrayal of all that the Church
has stood for within the national community.

It would, of course, be absurd to pretend that the pluralist
Britain of today could have a national Church fully able to
express the nation on its spiritual side. We ought rather to look
for a way of serving the nation equivalent, in the changed
circumstances of the time, to the service provided in the past.
Such a way is not to be found by withdrawing from all past
positions: bishops as lords spiritual, a chaplain to the Speaker
of the House, Remembrance Day, Industrial Sunday services,
and the like. We should rather be sensitive to new occasions
which present themselves. It was most appropriate, for
instance, that in 1975 the Archbishops of Canterbury and York
issued a Call to the Nation in their own names and not in that
of the British Council of Churches.

It may be, however, that the Church has retreated so far

from the points of actual national concern that she can no longer fulfil more than the palest semblance of her historic role. If that be so, it is perhaps better for her to cut her losses and complete the change into one among so many denominations. I have no enthusiasm for such a course.

5

If Anglican opinion is prepared to admit that post-Conciliar Rome is now free of those elements which call for protest to the point of separation, efforts should be made to achieve unity at a corporate level.

A generation ago it seemed quite unrealistic even to consider the possibility of corporate reunion. Roman Catholics officially were prepared to accept that anyone baptized in the threefold Name was a Christian, and as such belonged ultimately to the Church. But if he belonged to a Protestant body (a category which included the Church of England), that membership did little or nothing to advance his sanctification. Its ministry and its sacraments were no true ministry and sacraments; and though God in his mercy might bestow blessings through them, such blessings were exceptional and uncovenanted mercies.

Many Catholics, it is true, regretted the position, and attempts were made to find some formula which might enable ecumenical relations to begin between Christian bodies as such as well as between Christian individuals. But Catholic theologians easily went too far and found themselves in trouble with the authorities. It was not until Pope John opened the Vatican windows that a breath of fresh air swept into official attitudes. One of the chief functions of the Council which he called was to promote Christian unity.

The decree on Ecumenism (*De Ecumenismo*)[38] is in some ways the most exciting of the Council's formal documents, for it breaks new ground. First, it endorsed and brought to the centre of Catholic concern the belief, fostered over the years especially by the work of Abbé Couturier at Lyon, that God's will was for unity and that prayer for it was a sharing in Christ's own prayer. Secondly, it made the revolutionary admission that schisms had come about through 'developments for which, at times, men of both sides are to blame';[39] hitherto the Catholic Church had found it impossible to accept a share in the guilt attaching to schism. Even more important was the discovery of an acceptable way of describing non-Catholic Christian bodies. 'Ecclesial communities' implies that those communities in themselves have a genuine share in 'Church-ness'. It enables the Catholic theologian to distinguish them from the 'separated Churches' of the East which, if only for historical reasons, are evidently in a different category from the Churches which left the Roman unity at the Reformation. In a note on the phrase, Father Abbott says

> Implicit in the use of these terms ... is the idea that the more a Church has of the essential structures of the Catholic Church, the more it approaches the ideal of the Church. On this institutional scale of measurement, some are more properly called Churches than others, and the Decree regards Eastern Churches as practically sister Churches of the Roman Catholic Church.[40]

Clearly, a huge new range of ecumenical possibilities has been opened. The Anglican–Roman Catholic International Commission already mentioned is one of many similar bodies that have come into existence. The terminology, the machinery, and the will to work for unity are now all present.

But how far and how fast and in what shape?

We saw earlier[41] that if Rome seemed to have purged herself of those errors which caused the divisions of the sixteenth century, those who valued Evangelical religion had two other questions. Have the claims which she makes for herself come to look inherently likely? And if they have, are they fulfilled in the Roman obedience as it is now developing? The answers to those questions will largely determine the kind of relationship with Rome which we seek.

This is not the place for adequate discussion of the matter. The place of the papacy in a reunited Church will rank high on the agenda of inter-confessional theological discussion for some years to come. Already there is no shortage of suggestions for such agenda, and in groups official and unofficial discussion has already advanced some way. It seems clear that theologians of many traditions are prepared at least to take seriously a 'Petrine office' as a necessary element in any universal Catholic ministry. It is possible to identify various separate factors which predispose Christians to consider the matter more favourably than they would have done a generation ago. Changes in the papal image and attitudes count for much. There is the need for a personal focus if any large organization is to inspire love and loyalty. There is disillusion over democracy in Church affairs, for what promised to establish a Christian consensus has too often led to politicking over ecclesiastical elections. There is the new willingness to look at the 'Petrine passages' in Scripture, at Peter's role in the Acts of the Apostles. It is the task of ecumenical theology to look at all these and many others, to evaluate them, to see where they show agreement, to bring them into focus and coherence.

The process is bound to be lengthy. Fortunately it is not such as to make everything else wait until it is complete. Indeed it is a process which can best be worked out alongside other matters. We do not have to decide upon the extent or the type of unity before working towards it. The Anglican–Roman Catholic International Commission seems to have shelved the question of goal, wisely deciding to work on the principle of *solvitur ambulando*. Opinions about the 'Petrine office' are likely indeed to change with greater familiarity. Increasingly, however, some variation on the theme of 'uniate' relationship is coming to the fore as one manner in which the Anglican communion might come into organic relationship with Rome; with or without one or more preliminary phases marked by deepening degrees of intercommunion and other sharing.

The advantages of mutual intercommunion (to be distinguished from one-sided hospitality) lies in assuring the bodies concerned that each accepts the other's Christian integrity and 'substantial orthodoxy' without endorsing all that they teach. A particular problem of the Anglican–Roman Catholic scene is the implication carried by intercommunion that the ministry of both Churches is technically all that it should be; a point which the Romans would find it harder than the Anglicans to agree. It is not, however, insoluble.

The disadvantage of intercommunion is that it might become a substitute for full unity, the two bodies being content to go on indefinitely enjoying sacramental fellowship without bothering to go further. Recent Christian history supplies sad examples of such arrested development.

Intercommunion might well be a stage on the road, marking a considerable degree of unity already realized, and symbolizing commitment to further joint advance. But even at its fullest level, intercommunion would still imply separate and parallel denominations, however amicable they were. It is one thing to have full communion between one national Church and another, but quite a different matter when it is between two international bodies which could expect to go on existing side by side in every sizeable town throughout the world.

Which is one reason why ecumenists are looking with growing interest at the uniate Churches.

Another reason is that uniate Churches keep their own traditions while acknowledging the Pope's position as St Peter's successor. There is, as has already been mentioned, a feeling developing among Protestant churchmen that the Papacy is desirable as a focus of unity. The problem is to discern the 'Petrine office' amid the trappings with which the accidents of history have decorated it.

The essence of uniate status is that a group of previously separated Christians enters the Roman communion by an agreement which safeguards its traditional language, rites, and canon law. The first two are of less importance to Anglicans now that Rome has adopted the vernacular and the Prayer Book services have been revised. The third makes the arrangement particularly attractive to Anglicans. Most of the existing uniate Churches derive from sections of the Greek, Russian, or Syrian Orthodox Churches which for various reasons, often political, entered the Roman obedience from the sixteenth century onwards.[42] They have been allowed to keep the married priesthood, which is a feature of the Orthodox Church. The attraction of that precedent for Anglicans is obvious.

It is more than a question of clerical convenience. The history of the parson's wife is interesting. Archbishop Cranmer became convinced that it was lawful for a priest to marry (Orthodox bishops, who are drawn from the monks, are not married) but had to conceal his belief from King Henry VIII. Queen Elizabeth shared her father's distaste for such ladies, and refused to meet the wife of her great Archbishop, Matthew Parker. In the next reign George Herbert, poet, country parson, and the author of *A Priest to the Temple*, a classic of Anglican ministry, much preferred his parson to be celibate.[43] Throughout the seventeenth century the ordinary parson's status in the community was not high and the parsonage lady of little account. It was not until the eighteenth century, when the parson often achieved equal standing with the squire in the local hierarchy, that the parson's wife could become that power which brought so much relief to the hard times of the nineteenth century. From that time until the middle of the present century the vicarage family held a position of great importance in parish life. Now that inflation has eaten away the parson's 'living' and his stipend has fallen behind that of any other graduate professional, the vicarage family is often an anomaly. Nevertheless it is an institution most characteristically Anglican. Most congregations want it, and in so doing show acute appreciation of one formative element in the tradition which they have received.

In allowing for a married priesthood, therefore, uniate status would not only allow many Anglican clergy to continue functioning within the Roman obedience, but would also be a most important means of permitting Anglican church life to flourish with a minimum of disturbance. Another factor of special importance to the more devout parishioners would be continued right to communicate in both kinds. There is also a host of minor matters which go to make up the distinctive 'ethos' of Anglicanism and would remain undisturbed by uniate status. The result would be not only to avoid the destruction of a distinctive style of church life which has proved capable of changing with changing times while maintaining its integrity, but also keep to a minimum the deep-seated English fear of popery, which is by no means dead.

Uniate status, it must not be forgotten, presupposes that the two parties concerned have gone a long way in accepting one another. The work of the Anglican–Roman Catholic International Commission is building up a body of agreed doctrine, uncovering in the process other areas for exploration, perhaps over many years. Many Anglican theologians have suggested programmes of theological clarification which will be needed for any serious *rapprochement* with Rome. It is worth considering briefly three.

Dr James Atkinson published *Rome and Reformation* in 1966.[44] It forms part of a series entitled 'Christian Foundation', which appeared under the auspices of the Evangelical Fellowship of the Anglican Communion. He asks the question, 'Can Roman Catholicism so reform itself as to take Protestantism into its system?' and offers a programme whose satisfactory completion could lead to an affirmative answer. It

> will mean the examination of the evangelical doctrine of salvation by Christ alone apart from works or merit, and its relation to the Roman scheme of redemption. It will mean a re-examination of the doctrine of the priesthood of all believers and a reassessment of the role of clergy and laity in the Church; the bitter attack on the mediatorial, sacrificing priesthood; the whole doctrine of the mass, transubstantiation, masses for the dead, purgatory, indulgences and the centrality of the mass in Roman Catholic theology and practice.[45]

The list is long; it includes justification by faith ('a doctrine very nearly assimilated by Cardinal Contarini in his desire to reform the Church and retain the Lutherans'), Scripture and tradition, Christology and Mariology; but 'perhaps the doctrine of the Church will prove the hardest struggle, nevertheless the hierarchic Roman view must be examined in the light of the purely biblical view of the Reformers.'[46] Interestingly, Atkinson insists that Anglicanism itself must set its own house in order by a return to its Reformation norms.

The estimate of Emmanuel Amand de Mendieta is rather

different. He too insists that Anglicanism itself has a work of inner clarification to perform before decisive conversations with Rome would prove useful; but he seeks not a return to Reformation standards but a dialectical process which would change the relation of Protestant and Catholic elements in Anglicanism 'from symbiosis to synthesis'.[47] In his book *Anglican Vision*[48] he develops that thesis in the light of the Vatican II documents. His assessment has particular interest in that he had been a well-known Roman Catholic priest and scholar. Having become an Anglican in 1956, he was much concerned to further unity with Rome. He saw the process of 'synthesis' proceeding by the interaction of several pairs of complementary truths: justification by faith and the sacraments; Holy Scripture and the doctrinal tradition of the Church; the Church as mystery and as institution.[49]

Professor John Macquarrie proposed the only one of the three programmes which has in view a specifically uniate solution to Anglican–Roman Catholic relations. In his book *Christian Unity and Christian Diversity*[50] he lists five *Quaestiones Disputatae* which demand attention. Four of them he regards as on the way to solution: ministry, Eucharist, marriage, and Mariology. The fifth, authority, he finds much harder.

Dr de Mendieta and Dr Macquarrie both start from a Catholic position with regard to the basic nature of the Church, seeing the 'Protestant principle' as that which questions the 'Catholic substance'. (Macquarrie employs that distinction of Tillich, de Mendieta does not.) Dr Atkinson on the other hand is an Evangelical greatly influenced by Luther, on whom he is a leading authority. Those facts indicate the strength of their respective treatment of the subject, and also the limitations of their appeal. Further, all three are writing essentially in dogmatic terms. We should not neglect difficult matters on the borderline between 'doctrine' and 'discipline' which affect the ordinary lay Christian who is innocent of theology, and which so powerfully shape the 'ethos' of a Church. Artificial birth-control is an obvious example.

Any uniate arrangement would almost certainly disrupt the Church of England and the Anglican Communion. Those

Anglicans who considered the original Reformation protests as still needed would presumably not take part. They might form themselves into a continuing body; conceivably, such are the complexities of the law, they might find much property vested in them. Others might join another Protestant body. Protestants of a radical kind might also prefer not to join; as might indeed more Catholic-minded Anglicans who feel that the papacy is a serious distortion of Catholic truth. It is nevertheless hard to see any other solution to the problem of Christian unity in which the Church of England as a whole would agree to take part. Nor is it possible to maintain the *status quo*. Virtue and integrity have gone out of Anglicanism as it now is; to do nothing will lead to stagnation and atrophy.

Thus far I have written of Anglicanism as an Anglican. I have discussed the acceptability of uniate status and, with arrogance, the acceptability of Rome. But the very notion is the merest pipedream unless the Roman authorities were to find the Anglican world acceptable. It could well be that they would only be able to do so after the exclusion of the more Protestant views. For that reason also uniate status might be achieved only at the price of disrupting the Church of England.

On the other hand, some of those whom I called relative Protestants will feel that the Roman renewal has taken away the need for Reformation in the old sense. In that case, they might well be prepared to accept a 'rounding up' into more Catholic form of aspects of the faith where they had before insisted on a Protestant version. Anomalies and embarrassments might indeed result. A clergyman ordained on a Protestant understanding of his calling, for instance, would be in a delicate position if he found it right to accept a Catholic view of those things but lacked a sense of being called to fulfil them. Integrity might demand that he retire into lay Catholic communion.

One negative result of an Anglican Uniate Church would come from the resolution of previous Anglican tensions. The possibilities for reunion as a meeting-place between Catholic and Evangelical would have gone. Two reflections, however, pull in different directions. The Church of England's record as a reconciling Church has been most disappointing; and we have yet to experience the reconciling power generated when symbiosis has fully turned to synthesis.

6

Conclusions

I have considered elements which go to make up the unity and the variety of human life, here and hereafter, as the Christian faith describes it. The book must have an end, but there is no end to its subject. It would be foolish, therefore, to claim any sort of completeness for what I have written. More needs to be said on every one of the foregoing themes, by way of balance, extension, and, no doubt, correction. I wrestled long with a title for this chapter and fell back on the most pedestrian. Even so, a wise qualification would be the adjective 'provisional'. He who writes on such subjects is like a man who stands on a broad mist-covered mountain. Here and there the mist lifts to show something of the ground and its contours, another peak some miles away and other glimpses elsewhere. He takes his bearings from what he sees, matching direct sight with compass and map. He draws what he sees. But the sketchbook of his friend half a mile to the south and two hundred feet higher will show the same ground differently. How amusing it will be to compare notes when the mist has wholly lifted!

Human life stretches from here to eternity. It is the life of a spiritual animal responding to its Creator in primal simplicity; then, floundering and confused, damaged, the victim of its own misused potential; finally restored into the image of its Creator who had himself taken on its form. It is successively a glory of one kind, a shame, and a glory of another kind.

Mankind is a unity. That is the chief thing to grasp. The unity of the species is a unity marked by an inner difference, for it reflects the unity of the Creator who is One and Three. Human unity is composed of the harmonious and constructive functioning of millions and millions of separate parts. These are the persons who make up humanity.

The pattern of human existence is that of a glory of one kind, a shame, and a glory of another kind. The pattern marks the individual, and it marks every social grouping in which individuals have ever been found. When it does not follow through to the second glory, human life is tragic. It is pitiful to see how often today people get stuck in the shame and never see through to the glory beyond. Only the stubbornest optimism can survive a belief that human life stops with the death of the body.

The destiny of the species and the destiny of the individual alike belong with Christ who is the centre of mankind.

We looked into that earlier by following the biblical clue of Adam. Adam, we say, figures in the inspired presentation as Everyman, an individual and the species as a whole. It helps to consider the destiny of man in terms of Adam and Christ. Jesus the Christ is the man from God who overcame evil, thus removing the sting of death. He is the New Adam, standing undamaged before God as in the old myth the first man did before he fell to temptation. But the New Man has passed through temptation and put it firmly behind him.

Christ the New Man is the nucleus of the new humanity. A dozen biblical images show him gathering his people around him, welding them into one, living out his own life in them, among them; enlarging his Body with each new generation. At first almost all the members of his Body were in this life. Stephen's was the first recorded death, and he went to the same Jesus who a short time later was living in the brethren at Damascus whom Saul was about to arrest.

Later, the proportions began to change (so far, that is, as we in this life still can tell; there is more than a hint that he had his following also among the dead from Old Testament times); and the dead among whom Christ was living became a great multitude whom no man can number from all tribes and peoples and tongues. They have since expanded wonderfully, thus enlarging the total Christ, and so it goes on until the end of time.

The message to the living is evident. 'Thou wast not born for death, immortal bird', sang Keats to the nightingale;

'No hungry generations tread thee down.' Nor, had he but known it, do they tread us down. The unity of mankind in Adam and Christ is part of the gospel, which means that it is good news. We are not crushed into oblivion by the remorseless march of history. For the tremendous Body which the generations continue to build up is no faceless crowd. Individual human beings are not squeezed and pulped into some abstraction called humanity. Beyond our powers of imagination though it may be, that immensity which is being constructed is a community of individuals each of whom reaches personal fulfilment in an articulation by love. That was clear to the first Christian generation:

> We are to grow up in every way into him who is the head, into Christ, from whom the whole body, joined and knit together by every joint with which it is supplied, when each part is working properly, makes bodily growth and upbuilds itself in love.[1]

Of course, not every part works properly here and now; hence the need for the clinic called purgatory.

So much for Adam the species. Turning to Adam the individual, we see how each personality is preserved in the particular love of Christ. He is not only the life which informs the human race; he also lives through each separate individual. It is because the same life exists on the grand scale through the constantly increasing total humanity, even down to the newest and tiniest child, that the individual is not overwhelmed but on the contrary comes to personal fruition.

There is, so I have heard, a certain religious order the members of which are accustomed to genuflect not only to the Blessed Sacrament but also to each other after receiving Holy Communion, for Christ is dwelling in each of them.

2

Thus far we have considered the human race as a whole, and the individuals who make it up without distinctions between them. The discussion has been in Christian terms, concerned with Christ and his Body. But is not that to speak exclusively, since only a minority in each generation is Christian? There are millions who have never heard; and of those who do hear, very many reject or fail to respond. Are there then only few that be saved?

Logic would suggest so. There are, too, many scriptural passages that suggest it, among them some which go back to the direct authority of the Lord himself. Yet the Christian conscience by and large has found it intolerable and has sought a dozen ways round it. Against nature's amazing waste at almost all levels of animal and vegetable life, Christians have dwelt on the solidarity of mankind, on the extent to which the part may act on behalf of the whole. We said earlier that you had to opt out rather than to opt in.

Yet the Church has never endorsed a full-blooded doctrine of universal salvation. That would seem to be the most merciful course; but two factors cast doubt on whether it would be so merciful after all.

It is often said that the final loss of one soul would sour the joy of all those who are saved. 'That sounds very merciful' says the Teacher in one of C. S. Lewis's allegories.

> But see what lurks behind it ... The demand of the loveless and the self-imprisoned that they should be allowed to black-mail the universe: that till they consent to be happy (on their own terms) no one else shall taste joy: that their's should be the final power; that Hell should be able to *veto* Heaven.[2]

The other factor is the courtesy of grace. Grace treats people seriously, with respect for their integrity. Grace, we saw earlier, does not pauperize; nor does it override human decision. That supreme act of grace, the redemption of the world, waited upon the Blessed Virgin's decision. Grace will move the human spirit by every means except one; it will not storm the inmost citadel of a personality which is finally closed. There comes a point where love can only accept rejection.[3]

A point which emerges from this discussion is the great importance of personal decision. Further, Catholic and Protestant teaching agree in the importance of the present life as the theatre of final decision. That fact makes it impossible to suppose that this present life is insignificant in anything except its duration. Indeed, the shortness of an earthly life-span increases its importance, for eternal consequences are concentrated into its few years. This world is indeed a 'vale of soul-making',[4] unaware though people may be of the process in which they are engaged. The vital thing being forged is a basic cast of spirit, a direction, a tendency either for or against life. Sooner or later it will be focussed in a response for or against Christ, the Lord of life.

To call that 'something' the will is misleading if it is taken to imply that the 'something' is always conscious. A person's basic will may be so muddled or muffled by circumstances that it is hardly to be discerned in the pattern of his actions. It is a matter where we are warned not to judge. But even where it is only embryonic, it is still there, for without it one is less than a human person. Everyone basically is pointing in a certain direction and sooner or later that direction will be made known.

> Once to every man and nation
> comes the moment to decide,
> In the strife of Truth with Falsehood,
> for the good or evil side.[5]

Nothing that we have written, therefore, lessens the Church's duty to preach the gospel to every creature. The implicit Christian must be given the chance to become explicit, the latent to rise into action, the anonymous to learn his true name. The great English puritan Richard Baxter speaks for all Christian witness:

> I preached as never sure to preach again,
> And as a dying man to dying men![6]

Yet our preaching (and equivalent activities) should be done with humility. We cannot be sure that words reach the hearer with the message intended when they were uttered. The hearer's experience may cause them to ring quite different bells. We should therefore be slow to draw negative conclusions from failure to respond; we do not know the whole story. It is no human advocacy but the Spirit of the Lord that enables the true confession of Jesus.

3

Contemplating eternal issues, it is easy to fall into the snare of discounting time. The destiny of mankind in God's purpose is heady stuff and can make us look patronizingly at human institutions. In those soaring perspectives, what can be the virtue of earthly thrones and governments? If eternity be our home, does time matter?

Contempt for the world endangers the human soul, for it ministers to pride. It is very different from contentment with our earthly lot in view of heavenly treasures. One should approach the martyrs with caution. True martyrdom is never self-imposed. Those who know themselves to be a colony of heaven[7] should take seriously the present world, for it too is the Lord's.

That caution is needed nowhere more urgently than in church affairs. Evangelicals in particular, whose turn of belief makes them notably assured of salvation, too often sit light to obligations of church order. One has heard the Church of England extolled as 'the best boat to fish from'.

A sociological account of the Church is not always easily matched with the theological description. But it is necessary to bring the two into relation unless the faith is to float off into a spirituality unearthed in historical structures; and that cannot be allowed among followers of the Word made flesh. The unspirituality and worldliness of much church life is not to be commended, but at least it can be a reminder of him through whom Christians worship.

The visible Church will no doubt fall into the background when the Kingdom of God lies open to sight; but until then it is all that we have as a sign of what will be. In that day denominational differences may linger for a moment in the memory as a sick joke. They are now of capital importance: against the Lord's will, a stumbling block to many within the churches and to more beyond them, a waste of time and money, of energy and loyalty.

The chapter in this book devoted to the Church militant was written from an Anglican standpoint, and within the Anglican spectrum it started from a broadly Evangelical position. I concluded that, if an independent Anglican presence is to be maintained usefully, it will stress the Protestant elements in its inheritance of reformed Catholicism. I do not believe that the 'non-papal Catholicism', which appears to be the practical ideal towards which Anglicanism has been tending for most of a century, is valuable enough to preserve at the cost of maintaining the separation from Rome.

My conclusions may well cause irritation or sadness, which I regret. But even if they are rejected, I insist upon the underlying concern: that a theological description of the Church in terms of God's purpose for mankind has not been properly made without bringing it into relation with the actual state of divided Christendom.

4

In the year of our Lord 627 Edwin, king of Northumbria, held a council of his great men. Their business was to decide whether to abandon the old religion in favour of Christianity. Queen Ethelberga was already a Christian, and her counsellor Bishop Paulinus had come to court with her as a missionary to the King and his people. The King hesitated for some time, during which Paulinus was able to preach and to teach unhindered. Then came the fateful Council.

The high priest, Coifi, said that all his faithful service of the old gods had brought him no reward; and, having heard Paulinus, his vote was for change.

Another of the King's chief men agreed, but for different reasons. 'Your Majesty,' he said,

'when we compare the present life of man with that time of which we have no knowledge, it seems to me like the swift flight of a lone sparrow through the banqueting-hall where you sit in the winter months to dine with your thanes and counsellors. Inside there is a comforting fire to warm the room; outside, the wintry storms of snow and rain are raging. This sparrow flies swiftly in through one door and out through another. While he is inside, he is safe from the winter storms; but after a few moments of comfort, he

vanishes from sight into the darkness whence he came.
Similarly, man appears on earth for a little while, but we
know nothing of what went before this life, and what follows.
Therefore if this new teaching can reveal any more
certain knowledge, it seems only right that we should follow
it.'[8]

And so, after a little more consideration, they did.

Modern theologians may say that it is not desirable; but
the concern to be reassured, which led King Edwin's nameless
counsellor to advise acceptance of the Christian faith, remains
compelling. Certainly it is and has always been a prominent
element in Evangelical religion. As we have seen, however, fear
of Catholic excess has prevented many Evangelicals from finding
the fulfilment of their assurance in belonging to that
community of love which transcends death. Their fellowship
with the departed has remained stunted, a formal belief only.
Wishing above all to make much of Christ and their salvation
in him, they have underestimated the solidarity of which he is
the nucleus. They have drawn a line between Christ and the
saints, where they should have realized he is to be known and
met through the saints who form part of his Body.

Part of the gospel celebration is that human beings find
themselves in the end to be in very good company. The life of
man, despite any appearances in the here-and-now, is not
'solitary, poor, nasty, brutish and short'. The New Testament
writer saw further into things than did Thomas Hobbes.

> You have come to Mount Zion and to the city of the
> living God, the heavenly Jerusalem, and to innumerable
> angels in festal gathering, and to the assembly of the first-
> born who are enrolled in heaven, and to a judge who is God
> of all, and to the spirits of just men made perfect, and
> to Jesus, the mediator of a new covenant, and to the
> sprinkled blood that speaks more graciously than the blood
> of Abel.[9]

One has the impression that his mind stumbles in the attempt
to speak of such richness. It is the richness of the good company
into which he and his readers have been introduced.

Another New Testament letter expresses the same message in different imagery, and a less breathless tone leads to more orderly presentation. Christians are not to allow themselves to be blown off course 'by every wind of doctrine, by the cunning of men, by their craftiness in deceitful wiles'; or, as we might say, by the current intellectual fad.

> Rather, speaking the truth in love, we are to grow up in every way into him who is the head, into Christ, from whom the whole body, joined and knit together by every joint with which it is supplied, when each part is working properly, makes bodily growth and upbuilds itself in love.[10]

The process of articulation is one and the same on both sides of the chasm known as the death of the body. Reflection upon the implications of that great passage in Paul's Letter to Ephesus will enable the Evangelical theologian to find his distinctive insight into Christian truth completed in the Catholic doctrine of the communion of saints. It will enable Evangelical Christians whether or not they are theologians to find release and joy in discovering that their salvation has admitted them into such good company.

Notes and Indexes

Notes

CHAPTER 1 THE STARTING POINT

[1] S.P.C.K. 1976.
[2] Eng.tr. *To Honour Mary*. C.T.S. 1974.
[3] W. M. Abbott, S. J. and J. Gallagher, ed., *The Documents of Vatican II*. Geoffrey Chapman 1967; (hereafter cited as *Docs Vat II*), p. 13.
[4] James Boswell, *The Life of Samuel Johnson*, LLD, ed. G. B. Hill, rev. L. F. Powell, 6 vols. (O.U.P. 1934–64), vol. iii, p. 273.
[5] Rev. 7.9. Unless otherwise stated, biblical texts are cited from the Revised Standard Version.
[6] L. S. Thornton, *The Common Life in the Body of Christ*. Dacre Press 1942.

CHAPTER 2 THE EDGES OF MYSTERY

[1] Joseph Addison, *The Spectator* no. 465.
[2] *Anglicanism* (Penguin Books 1958), p. 263.
[3] From speech delivered at Oxford at a meeting of the Society for Increasing Endowments of Small Livings in the Diocese of Oxford, 25 November 1864. Quoted by Neill, op. cit., p. 264.
[4] John Osborne, *Luther*. Faber & Faber 1961.
[5] Martin Esslin, *The Theatre of the Absurd*. Penguin rev. edn 1968.
[6] *Leviathan*, 1.13.
[7] *Christian Believing* (S.P.C.K. 1976), p. 10.
[8] *The Christian Universe* (Darton, Longman & Todd 1960), pp. 47–8.
[9] Ibid., p. 48.
[10] *The Reason Why*, 1926; reprinted with *The Catholic Church and Conversion* (Burns & Oates 1960), p. 103.
[11] *Ring of Truth* (Hodder & Stoughton 1967), p. 38.
[12] Pelican Books 1971.
[13] Neill, loc. cit., p. 264.
[14] E. L. Mascall, ed., hereafter cited as *ALPD*. Faith Press 1954.
[15] Ibid., p. 62.
[16] Heb. 13.2.
[17] *ALPD*, p. 12.
[18] Ibid., p. 13.
[19] Cf. Hodges in *ALPD*, p. 15.
[20] Ibid.
[21] (Faith Press 1962), pp. 110–11.

[22] *Four Quartets* (Faber 1944), p. 36.
[22] Kenneth Grahame, *The Wind in the Willows* (Methuen 38th. edn 1931), p. 161.
[24] Ibid., p. 163.
[25] R. Otto, *The Idea of the Holy*, Eng.tr. O.U.P. 1923; Penguin 1959.
[26] W. Y. Fullerton, cited from *Christian Praise* (Tyndale Press 1957), p. 107.

CHAPTER 3   ADAM FROM FIRST TO LAST

[1] Ps. 8. 1 and 3–4.
[2] Ibid. 5–8.
[3] *A Catechism.*
[4] *Reflections in a Mirror*, 2nd series (Macmillan 1946), p. 146.
[5] Ibid., p. 147.
[6] Ibid.
[7] Ibid.
[8] Ibid., p. 148.
[9] See e.g. Alec R. Vidler, *The Theology of F. D. Maurice.* S.C.M. 1948; John Taylor, *Man in the Midst.* Highway Press 1955.
[10] Gen. 2.21–5.
[11] Ps. 139.7–10.
[12] See Gen. 6.1–4.
[13] Cf. Denys Hay, *Europe the Emergence of an Idea.* (Edinburgh University Press 1957), especially chapters 1 and 3.
[14] Matt. 5.1–2.
[15] John 6.70.
[16] Luke 2.32; cf. Acts 1.8.
[17] Acts 1.26.
[18] Matt. 19.28.
[19] Luke 22.28–9.
[20] 1 Cor. 15.22; cf. Rom. 5.12–17, 2 Cor. 5.17.
[21] Acts 9.1–5.
[22] 1 Cor. 7.25–32.
[23] 1 Cor. 7.17–24.
[24] 1 Thess. 4.13–18.
[25] 2 Cor. 5.1–10.
[26] Phil. 1.19–26.
[27] Col. 3.18–4.6; Eph. 5.21–6.9; 1 Peter 2.11–3.7.
[28] 2 Peter 3.8–10.
[29] Matt. 18.18–20.
[30] Acts 1.3.
[31] Acts 1.6–11.
[32] John 19.25–8.
[33] John 20.19–23.
[34] John 12.31–3.
[35] John 19.30.
[36] John 5.24.

37 *Hereafter* (Hodder & Stoughton and Christian Book Promotion Trust 1972), p. 89.
38 Ibid., pp. 92–3.
39 Hodges, *ALPD*, p. 13.
40 Winter, p. 37.
41 Ibid., p. 54.
42 Ibid., pp. 37–8.
43 Cited by Winter from an essay in *Inter-Varsity*, 1970.
44 1 Cor. 15.44.
45 Winter, p. 39.
46 Shaw in *ALPD*, p. 49.
47 Ibid.
48 Ibid., p. 51.
49 Ibid.
50 Ibid.
51 Ibid., p. 52.
52 S. Neill, *Anglicanism*, p. 264.
53 Gen. 21.13.
54 Ps. 51.12.
55 Luke 1.47 (Prayer Book).
56 C. F. D. Moule in *The Parish Communion Today*, ed. D. M. Paton (S.P.C.K. 1962), p. 84.
57 Gal. 5.22–3.
58 Heb. 12.2.
59 John 16.20–2.
60 Eph. 3.15.
61 Gal. 4.4–5.
62 Gal. 4.6.
63 C. F. Evans, *The Lord's Prayer* (S.P.C.K. 1963), p. 28.
64 1 Cor. 12.3.
65 Rom. 8.26–7.
66 Luke 20.34–6. Parallels are found at Matt. 22.29–31 and Mark 12.24–5.
67 I owe the argument in this particular form to H. A. Williams, *True Resurrection* (Mitchell Beazley 1972), chapter 3.
68 Eph. 4.15–16.
69 Matt. 25.31–46.
70 1 Cor. 15.24.

CHAPTER 4 JACOB'S LADDER

1 Notably in Vatican II's Decree on The Church (*De Ecclesia*; also known as *Lumen Gentium*), consideration of which underlies much of the present chapter.
2 Gen. 28.13–7.
3 Acts 7.54–6.
4 Acts 7.59–60.
5 Gen. 12.1–3.

6 Acts 7.52; cf. vv. 2–8.
7 Acts 7.55.
8 See above, pp. 46–7.
9 Shakespeare, *Hamlet* I. 5.166.
10 Shaw in *ALPD*, pp. 60–1.
11 Chatto–Heinemann for Sussex University Press 1975.
12 Cohn, p. 73.
13 1 John 3.8.
14 Shaw in *ALPD*, p. 61.
15 1 John 4.2–3.
16 1 Cor. 12.1–3.
17 Matt. 16.13–17.
18 *The Larger Catechism*, 1648, in T. F. Torrance, *The School of Faith* (James Clarke 1959), p. 185.
19 *ALPD*, p. 62.
20 237 Fulham Palace Road, Lodon SW6 6UB.
21 *Mary and the Christian Gospel*, S.P.C.K. 1976.
22 See also my paper *The Evangelical Mary* (Ecumenical Society of the Blessed Virgin Mary 1976, available from the Associate General Secretary, Campion Hall, Oxford, OX1 1QS).
23 Quoted in H. Graef, *Mary: A History of Doctrine and Devotion*, vol. i (Sheed & Ward 1963), p. 146.
24 Rom. 8.29–30.
25 *Mary and the Christian Gospel*, p. 79.
26 *To Honour Mary*. The apostolic exhortation *Marialis Cultus* of His Holiness Pope Paul VI 1974. C.T.S.
27 *Marialis Cultus*, 32.
28 Ibid., 33.
29 Ibid., 34.
30 Ibid., 35.
31 Ibid., 36.
32 Ibid., 37.
33 Ibid.
34 J. R. Lowell, *The Present Crisis*. University of Oregon Press 1941.
35 *Marialis Cultus*, 36.
36 Ibid., 38.
37 Ibid.
38 Ibid.
39 Ibid.
40 See my paper *The Evangelical Mary*, op. cit.
41 Phil. 2.12–13.
42 For a good, recent statement of traditional Anglican Evangelical teaching, see J. A. Motyer, *After Death* (Hodder & Stoughton 1965), especially chapter 5.
43 *De Ecclesia*, 49 (*Docs Vat II*, p. 80.)
44 Ibid., p. 78, note 225.

[45] *De Ecclesia*, 49.
[46] Ibid.
[47] *Docs Vat II*, p. 81.
[48] *De Ecclesia*, 50.
[49] Ibid., 51.
[50] See above, pp. 41–4.
[51] Matt. 18.10.
[52] Article 'Guardian angels' in F. L. Cross, ed., *Oxford Dictionary of the Christian Church* (O.U.P. 1957), p. 595.
[53] Acts 12.15.
[54] Luke 12.32.
[55] Rev. 8.2–4.
[56] Rev. 5.11–14.
[57] Rev. 7.9–12.
[58] I do not enter into the discussion of how far John's vision itself is clothed in images from the primitive Christian liturgy.

CHAPTER 5   MILITANT HERE IN EARTH

[1] Two books, very different from each other as well as from mine, are valuable as attempts to make sense of Catholic religion from Protestant standpoints. Pierre Yves Emery's *The Communion of Saints* Eng.tr. (Faith Press 1966) belongs by its subject more to the last chapter, though its historical method provides links with this one. F. J. Leenhardt's *Two Biblical Faiths* (Eng.tr. Lutterworth Press 1964) refers the characteristics of Protestant and Catholic theology to their underlying type of spirituality, the Protestant looking back to Abraham and the Catholic to Moses.
[2] See G. H. Williams, *The Radical Reformation* (1962) and select texts in G. H. Williams and A. M. Mergal, *Spiritual and Anabaptist Writers*. Library of Christian Classics, vol. XXV, S.C.M. 1957.
[3] A convenient modern edition is edited by J. E. Booty and published for the Folger Shakespeare Library by Cornell University Press, Ithaca, N.Y., 1963.
[4] See Pierre Janelle, *The Catholic Reformation*. The Bruce Publishing Co., Milwaukee, 1963.
[5] J. Atkinson, *Rome and Reformation* (Hodder & Stoughton 1966), pp. 53–4.
[6] Above pp. 70–1.
[7] Quoted from R. Kaiser, *Inside the Council* (Burns & Oates 1963), p. 83.
[8] Alan Clark and Colin Davey, ed., *Anglican/Roman Catholic Dialogue* (O.U.P. 1974), p. 68. The quotation is translated from *L'Eglise et les églises* (Chevetogne 1954), p. 258.
[9] The phrase occurs in *De Ecumenismo*, 11 (*Docs Vat II* p. 354).
[10] Ibid.
[11] *De Ecclesia*, 1 (*Docs Vat II*, p. 15).
[12] See e.g. H. Küng, K. Barth, O. Cullmann, and others, *Christianity Divided*. Sheed & Ward 1962.
[13] *De Revelatione*, 10 (*Docs Vat II* p. 117).

[14] Ibid. p. 118.

[15] Ibid.

[16] *Docs Vat II*, p. 132.

[17] *Difficulties felt by Anglicans in Catholic Teaching*, 4th edn., vol. i (Burns & Oates 1850), p. 378.

[18] Eph. 2.8.

[19] Op. cit., p. 403.

[20] Gerald B. Phelan in *The Sacred Heart of Jesus* by St John Eudes, tr. Dom Richard Flower, O.S.B., New York, P. J. Kenedy & Sons 1946.

[21] C. S. Lewis, *The Screwtape Letters* (Geoffrey Bles 1946), p. 85.

[22] Jean Guitton, *The Blessed Virgin*, Eng.tr. (Burns & Oates 1952), p. 3.

[23] Ibid., p. 4.

[24] *Quoted from La Pensée et le Mouvant*, p. 149.

[25] Op. cit., p. 5.

[26] Op. cit., p. 429.

[27] Philip Crowe, ed., *Keele '67* (Falcon Books 1967), p. 39.

[28] *The Holy Eucharist.* C.T.S. 1965.

[29] *Keele '67*, p. 39.

[30] Above, p. 103.

[31] J. Morris, ed., *New Ways with the Ministry.* Faith Press 1960.

[32] Ibid., p. 18.

[33] It is interesting to see how the new Church of England Canon C2 has acquired a theological gloss absent from the equivalent Canon 76 of 1603.

[34] Dacre Press 1947.

[35] ed. R. Newton Flew and Rupert E. Davies, Lutterworth Press 1950.

[36] S.P.C.K. 1950.

[37] The title of an essay by Howard Root in *Soundings*, ed. A. R. Vidler, C.U.P. 1962.

[38] Text in *Docs Vat II*, pp. 336–70. See also text with commentary by Bernard Leeming, S.J. in *The Vaticam Council and Christian Unity*. Darton, Longman & Todd 1966.

[39] *De Ecumenismo*, 3. See also the prayer for forgiveness in 7.

[40] *Docs. Vat. II*, p. 355.

[41] Above, p. 89.

[42] For a brief account of these bodies, see F. L. Cross, ed., *Oxford Dictionary of the Christian Church*, 2nd edn.

[43] *A Priest to the Temple*, 9.

[44] Hodder and Stoughton.

[45] *Rome and Reformation*, p. 81.

[46] Ibid., p. 82.

[47] See his essay of that title in *The Anglican Synthesis*, ed. W. R. F. Browning, Derby, Peter Smith, 1964.

[48] S.P.C.K. 1971.

[49] *Anglican Vision*, pp. 85–97.

[50] S.C.M. 1975.

Notes

CHAPTER 6 CONCLUSIONS

1 Eph. 4.15–16.
2 *The Great Divorce* (Geoffrey Bles 1946), p. 111.
3 George Adam Smith made the point classically in his commentary on Hosea, *The Book of the Twelve Prophets*, vol i, pp. 352–4 (The Expositor's Bible, Hodder & Stoughton) John A. T. Robinson put the opposite case powerfully in his *In the End, God* (James Clarke and Co. 1950), chs. 8–9. See especially the parable, pp. 122f.
4 John Keats *Letters*, ed. M. B. Forman 1935 (cited from *Oxford Dictionary of Quotations*, p. 290.)
5 J. R. Lowell, op. cit.
6 *Love Breathing Thanks and Praise*, part 2 (cited from *Oxford Dictionary of Quotations*, p. 36.)
7 James Moffatt's translation of Phil. 3.20. The Moffatt translation of the Bible is published by Hodder & Stoughton.
8 Bede, *A History of the English Church and People*, tr. Leo Shirley-Price (Penguin Books 1955), pp. 124f.
9 Heb. 12.22–4.
10 Eph. 4.15–16. If there is one single biblical passage from which the thesis of this book has grown, it is this.

Index of Names and Subjects

139

Index of Scripture References

Index of Scriptures References